Adoration in Spirit and Truth

Adoration in Spirit and Truth

Alain-Marie de Lassus, c.s.j.

But the hour is coming, and now is, when the true worshipers will worship the Father in spirit and truth, for such the Father seeks to worship him.

John 4:23

Adoration, ah! It's a name from Heaven!

St. Elizabeth of the Trinity

NEWMAN HOUSE PRESS

French Original: *Adorer en esprit et vérité*, Paris: Lethiélléux, 2010.
Copyright © Parôle et Silence. All rights reserved

English Translation: E. C. (Peter) Pitre
Copyright © Congregation of St. John. All rights reserved

This edition copyright © 2017 Newman House Press
601 Buhler Court, Pine Beach, New Jersey 08741

ISBN 978-0-9881888-7-7

Table of Contents

Introduction

The words "adoration," "adorable," and "adore" are particularly debased in our day and are often used in a sense very far from their original meaning. Let us quickly draw a few examples from everyday language:

"This child is adorable!"
By this, we mean that the child is cute and charming.

"I adore Chicago!" [1]
In other words, I am madly in love with that city.

In these examples, we are indeed far from the biblical concept of adoration, inasmuch as the essential relation of adoration to God has completely disappeared and the words are used in a purely profane sense. However, something important remains: the notion of great love.

Surely things are different in the Church, are they not? It is true that the terms connected with adoration are still used in connection with prayer and therefore with God. We must acknowledge, however, that not much is heard about adoration in the Church these days. Usually, when we do speak of it, it is only in reference to adoration of the Blessed Sacrament: adoring consists in kneeling before the Blessed Sacrament exposed on the altar and giving It homage.

---

[1] This phrase is taken from an advertisement for the city of Chicago that all Air France passengers heading for that city can see on board just before landing.

Adoration of the Blessed Sacrament is certainly an excellent practice, bearing much fruit in the Church today. It is nonetheless striking to observe that most Catholics seem to reduce adoration to adoration of the Blessed Sacrament and apparently do not see that its scope is a great deal broader than adoration of the Blessed Sacrament alone.

In this book, therefore, we will study adoration from the biblical, philosophical and theological points of view. A philosophical study of adoration may be surprising to some, but it is important, for it is essential to understand that adoration has a natural foundation. It is natural for the human person to adore God. The biblical study will gather together the major points of Sacred Scripture's teaching on adoration. Finally, the theological study will take a look at the essential role of adoration in the Christian life. In this way, we will follow the usual process of theological analysis, which always presupposes a philosophical foundation and then devotes itself to scrutinizing Scripture to elaborate its own reflection.

This study is composed of six chapters. We shall begin with a philosophical reflection on adoration as the natural love that human persons have for their Creator. Then we shall take a journey through the Bible on the theme of adoration, first in the Old Testament, then in the New. In the New Testament, we shall focus our attention on three passages: Jesus' conversation with the Samaritan woman (John 4), during which Jesus teaches adoration in spirit and truth, and chapters 4 and 13 of the Book of Revelation, which show, on the one hand, adoration in its perfection as it is lived in Heaven and, on the other, the idolatrous adoration of the Beast, who seeks to turn men away from adoring God. The fourth chapter is a theological reflection on the importance of adoration in the Christian life and the fruits produced by it in our lives. The fifth chapter will offer a few theological reflections on adoration of the

Blessed Sacrament. This chapter will not be the most developed, not because adoration of the Blessed Sacrament is of negligible importance for us—quite the contrary—but because it is much better known by the faithful. I shall conclude with a few practical points to help people unfamiliar with adoration to enter into this most fundamental prayer.

I shall illustrate the topic of adoration with citations from the Church's Magisterium and the writings of the saints, since it is the Church's saints who have lived adoration in spirit and truth most fully.

Chapter 1: Adoration As a Natural Human Act

This first part is an attempt to look at adoration philosophically. But is this possible? Does philosophy have something to say about adoration? Is it not it a matter for the theologian? This is doubtless a common idea today. However, if it is true that the philosopher is bound to take an interest in everything that touches man, because philosophers seek to know all the dimensions of man, then the philosopher cannot be ignorant of the religious dimension of the human person. It jumps out at us that in all the cultures of humanity and in all periods of history, man appears as a *religious being*. The phenomenon of atheism, as it has developed today, is a recent, relatively circumscribed phenomenon in human history. Its appearance can be dated to eighteenth-century Christian Europe, the period of the Enlightenment. No doubt there were atheists previously, but it seems they were few in number. Atheism emerged in Europe and developed during the age of the Enlightenment. It was not until nearly the nineteenth century that philosophical atheism appeared, by which I mean an atheism buttressed with philosophical arguments and justifications.[2] After Feuerbach, various sorts of atheism arose and spread, first in Europe, and then on other continents, but in the latter (and this point is noteworthy) it spread as an import, we might say, such as in China and North Korea, where atheism came through the influence of Marxism.

[2] Ludwig Feuerbach (1804–1872) seems to be the first. He exerted significant influence on Karl Marx.

Is this religious dimension, so universally present, an authentic dimension of the human person, or is it a deformation, an aberration? The philosopher must ask this question. Feuerbach considered God to be merely a sort of ideal projection of humanity onto a purely imaginary other. According to him, when people attribute to God the traditional perfections of eternity, omnipotence, and so on, they are only projecting outside of themselves attributes that in fact belong to humanity, attributes that humanity must take back for itself. Marx thought that religion was the opium of the people, by which the ruling classes attempted to lull the proletariat into greater exploitation. Freud, for his part, felt religion to be an illusion caused by the need of humanity, still at an infantile stage, to have a father; humanity had to leave behind this infantile stage to become fully mature by cutting this illusory umbilical cord.

The philosopher has to seek what may be true or erroneous in all of this. Clearly, it is crucial to know whether God exists, for that knowledge changes a great deal in one's life! This is not easy to do, however. Although the question of God (or the gods) is an ancient one in philosophy,[3] it is one of the most difficult in philosophical research, inasmuch as the existence of God is not immediately evident to human intelligence. This question is naturally of capital importance, but it cannot be first in the genetic order of philosophical research, that is, in the philosopher's research itinerary, at least not from a perspective of realistic philosophy.[4]

---

[3] It may even be said that it is the most ancient question in the history of philosophy, along with the question of the origin of the physical universe. It has been asked since the birth of philosophy in Greece.

[4] Realistic philosophy is the philosophical approach that seeks to know man starting from sense experience, and not from ideas. Aristotle initiated this way of philosophizing.

It is beyond the bounds of this book to expound in detail on the realistic way of doing philosophy in all its parts, as well as the manner in which, at the end of its itinerary, it approaches the question of God (for such a detailed inquiry, the reader can refer to philosophical studies on the question).[5] This ultimate stage of philosophical research is called *philosophical wisdom* or *natural theology*. *Wisdom* is the search for the first principles, and consequently for the highest, and therefore the ultimate, viewpoint on reality. Natural theology is a research about God or the gods (hence the noun "theology"[6]), but one that does not appeal to any revelation (hence the adjective "natural"). Natural theology uses metaphysics, the study of what exists inasmuch as it exists. At the end of a journey of intellectual research, the philosopher is led to conclude, not that God exists, but that a First Being exists.[7] Let us put this discovery in precise terms. The name "God" comes from human religious traditions. What the philosopher discovers is that, beyond all the existing realities that can be experienced, there necessarily exists an absolutely First Being, and the philosopher understands that this Being corresponds to the one men call by the name of God.

This First Being is discovered as a necessary, eternal being, a pure spirit existing beyond time, perfect and infinite in its being, whose life is blessed.[8]

[5] For the presentation of a contemporary, realistic philosophical itinerary, see for example *Retracing Reality* by Marie-Dominique Philippe (complete references of works cited are to be found at the end of this book).

[6] The word "theology," as an intellectual reflection or discourse (*logos*) about the divinity (*theos*), appeared in Greek philosophy with Plato, and so, well before Christianity. Several Greek philosophers, including Plato and Aristotle, developed reflections on natural theology.

[7] For a contemporary reflection on philosophical wisdom, see in particular Marie-Dominique Philippe's *De l'être à Dieu. De la philosophie première à la sagesse*, as well as his *Retour à la source*, volume II, *De la science à la sagesse*.

[8] This corresponds to the metaphysical discovery of the First Being as "pure act," that is (briefly), an absolutely perfect being in every respect, a being which

CREATION

After studying[9] the First Being in himself, as far as this is possible, the philosopher asks the question of the relationship between this First Being and other existing realities, man in particular. This is the problem of creation.[10] The philosopher discovers that all the realities other than the First Being are second in existence and depend on him ontologically. They are "created", which means that they receive their existence from the First Being. This conclusion is of great importance for the question of adoration: we do not exist by ourselves, but we receive our existence from the First Being. We say "we receive," not "we have received," for creation is not an act in the past for us, one that took place once for all at the beginning of our lives: at every instant of our existence, the First Being communicates being to us; he bears us in being, so to speak. More precisely, creation is not situated at the level of becoming, but of being. Understanding creation at the level of becoming is a rather common error. We find it in Voltaire, for example. He believed in God's existence because he could not conceive the universe "working" right without having been "set up" by someone: "The universe embarrasses me, and I cannot think that this watch exists and

possesses all the ontological perfections of the other realities, but in a mode of absolute simplicity. I must immediately clarify that one reaches the conclusion of the existence of this pure act, but one has no direct experience of it, for the First Being is not the object of immediate sense experience, and all the realities we experience are imperfect in their being. The first philosopher to have discovered the First Being as pure act was Aristotle (see *Metaphysics* XII.7).

[9] This "study" is more a contemplation, inasmuch as the First Being, being absolutely simple, cannot be analyzed.

[10] Historically speaking, the problem of creation was not developed by Greek philosophy before Christianity, not even by Aristotle in an explicit way (at least in Aristotle's extant writings). Philosophical reflection on creation was strongly spurred on by Christian theology.

have no watchmaker."[11] In this mechanical conception of the universe, God's role is analogous to a watchmaker's—once he has made the clock and put it in place, it works fine all by itself. It is supposed to be the same for the universe: God created the universe at the beginning and gave it an initial nudge to set it in movement; since then, the universe has worked just fine by itself and has no need of God. In a different way, we find the same lack of distinction between the levels of being and becoming in the works of some contemporary physicists who think the Big Bang theory enables man to put his finger on creation. According to this cosmological theory, the universe began about fifteen billion years ago with the explosion of an extremely small, dense primordial sphere from which all physical bodies draw their origin. Whatever the scientific validity of this theory, creation is not situated at some supposed primordial instant. Once again, creation is *at the level of being*. Whatever the manner in which the universe began in time, it remains dependent actually, in the here and now, on the Creator in its being.[12] If this dependence were to cease, the universe would immediately disappear into nothingness.

Creation is not a past event, but something present right now. We depend here and now on the Creator in our being. Understanding this ought not in any way be a source of angst, as though there were a danger that the Creator might either "forget" to keep us in existence or decide to "drop" us into nothingness. This is a totally imaginary fear. To get a grasp of this, we have to under-

[11] Voltaire, *Satires, Les cabales*, in *Oeuvres complètes*, volume II, Paris, 1843, p. 748.

[12] An analogous remark might be made about the theory of evolution in biology. This theory is situated at the level of becoming and not of being. Whatever may be the concrete historical manner in which the various living bodies appeared, they remain dependent on the Creator at the level of being.

stand the reason the Creator creates us. Philosophers have put forth various opinions on this subject that are interesting to know. Plotinus,[13] for example, thought that the first principle must necessarily beget, for this is proper to the perfect living being. Therefore, if God is perfect, then it is obvious that he must necessarily beget. But is this principle exactly true? Although it is true that an animal reaches the perfect stage of its biological development when it becomes able to reproduce another animal of its own species, does this principle apply to a purely spiritual being? Nothing permits us to affirm it. Creation is necessary for Hegel as well but in a different sense: according to Hegel, if God did not create, he would remain a purely abstract God, a God not yet fully conscious of his essence and possibilities. In creating something other than himself, God becomes aware of what he is and concretely becomes himself. Actually, if we have discovered the First Being as an absolutely perfect reality in his being, we understand that he does not need to create in order to develop his consciousness of himself. He is eternally perfect and fully lucid about his own perfection.

By contrast, these philosophical errors about creation help us understand better the wholly gratuitous nature of creation. If the First Being gives us existence, it is not that he needs to; it is not a necessity for him, but rather pure gratuitousness, which can only be explained by love. In other words, God creates us out of love, though he does not need us, not even to serve him, for he has no need of servants. What service could we possibly render him? Creation is therefore an entirely gratuitous act on God's part. "Gratuitous act" does not mean an arbitrary or capricious one. Creation is not a game, properly speaking; it is a serious act involving God's creative wisdom and all his goodness.

---

[13] Plotinus was a Neo-Platonic philosopher of the third century B.C.

ADORATION OF THE CREATOR

As brief as they are, these preliminary philosophical reflections were necessary to understand adoration, to which we now come. What is adoration, then, from a philosophical point of view? We can say that it is *the creature's natural love for his Creator*. However, if we wish to analyze it more deeply, we can distinguish four aspects in adoration:

First, *acknowledgement* of the Creator as such and therefore the recognition of the actual bond making man ontologically dependent on him. This is an act of intelligence acknowledging him as the Creator.

Second, *free, loving acceptance* by man of this dependence.[14]

Third, *thanksgiving* to the Creator for the gift of existence and all our natural gifts, beginning with our intelligence and will (our spirit).

Fourth, the *spiritual offering* to the Creator of all that we are. This offering may also take concrete form by material offerings, as we in fact see in various world religions. For example, the offering of the fruits of the earth is a gesture by which man recognizes that the nature in which he lives and that gives him its fruit is also created by God. Man receives it from the Creator through nature and benefits

---

[14] In current definitions of adoration, the aspect of acknowledgement is usually the one mentioned. For Bossuet, for example, adoration is the "acknowledgement in God of the highest sovereignty, and in us of the deepest dependence" (see Sermon on the worship of God, Friday of the third week of Lent, 1666, cited in "Adoration", *Encyclopédie Catholicism*, I, c. 157). Acknowledgement of God as the Creator is certainly fundamental to adoration, but we must not forget the love that is just as essential. Without love, total dependence on God would be very difficult to bear. Philosophical analysis must distinguish the act of intelligence that knows the First Being as the Creator from the act of will that loves, but, in the human person's life, these two are intimately bound together and *must not be separated*.

from it for his life. It is therefore right that man should express his gratitude to the Creator for these gifts.

An analogy drawn from human experience, that of the child's natural love for his mother, can help us understand the profound naturalness of adoration. We all understand that it is normal for children to love their mothers. Seeing a child who did not love his mother would raise questions within us: "Why is it that this child does not love his mother? What happened to make him not love her? This child must have been emotionally wounded. Was he perhaps rejected by his mother at some point?" We consider it normal for children to love their mothers for the simple reason that a mother is the source of life for her children. She communicated her human life to her children, in co-operation with the father. This communication of life constitutes a natural foundation explaining children's love for their mothers. This love can move us, but it does not surprise us, since it is natural.

We can reason analogously in our relationship with God. God communicates existence to us. This communication constitutes the foundation of a natural love for God. This natural love is adoration. It is therefore natural to love God as the source of our existence. We need to understand that communicating existence is something deeper and more radical than communicating life. Our parents communicated life to us, but God communicates to us our existence. God alone can do this, for he is the Creator.

From this we can draw out several consequences. First, adoration is reserved for the Creator, since he alone communicates existence. Of course, in everyday language we sometimes use the verb "to adore" for anything but God, as we said at the beginning. We say, for example, "I adore chocolate mousse," or "I adore the music of Wagner." By this we mean an intense love, sensible or aesthetic love, for chocolate mousse or Wagner's music. But it is clear that in these cases we are not using the word "adore" in its specific sense. We know that, fortunately! If, on the contrary, we wish to speak precisely, we must say that adoration is a love reserved for God, because it is love for the Creator. We will come upon this point once again in our biblical reflection on Christian adoration. Although other persons may be objects of veneration, such as the Virgin Mary, the saints and the angels, God alone is the object of adoration, properly speaking.

Second, if adoration is man's natural love for God the Creator, then we understand that, contrary to the assertions of atheistic philosophers, *man is naturally a religious being*. This explains why the efforts of totalitarian atheistic regimes to rout out religion from the human heart are vain and inevitably bound to fail. Orientation toward God is naturally rooted in the inmost depths of the human heart. Seeking to remove this orientation from the human heart blocks the development of an authentic dimension of the human person.

We have seen that adoration is founded on man's dependence on God the Creator and that creation is on God's part a free act of love. But is this dependence acceptable? Some contemporary atheistic philosophers, such as Sartre, consider it unacceptable. According to them, it would be unacceptable for man to have to depend on another reality to exist. This dependence would be a veritable alienation for man. If man is truly free, he cannot depend on another. Creatureliness would contradict authentic human freedom. To illustrate this claim, let us quote the dialogue from Sartre's *The Flies*:

ZEUS: Orestes, I created you, and I created all things. Now see . . . .

ORESTES: Let the rocks revile me, and flowers wilt at my coming. Your whole universe is not enough to prove me wrong. You are the king of gods, king of stones, and stars, king of the waves of the sea. But you are not king of man. (*The walls draw together. Zeus comes into view, tired and dejected, and he now speaks in his normal voice.*)

ZEUS: Impudent spawn! So I am not your king? Who, then, made you?

ORESTES: You. But you blundered; you should not have made me free.

ZEUS: I gave you freedom that you might serve me.

ORESTES: Perhaps. But now it has turned against its giver. And neither you nor I can undo what has been done. . . .

Neither slave nor master. I am my freedom. No sooner had you created me than I ceased to be yours. . . .

For I, Zeus, am a man, and every man must find out his own way. . . .

We shall glide past each other, like ships in a river, without touching. You are God and I am free; each of us is alone, and our anguish is kin.[15]

Two remarks may be made on this subject. First of all, Sartre's position may be considered as lacking truth, for we know very well that our freedom, though real, is not absolute. We do not have the means to do absolutely everything we would like to do; we are limited in our being and in our possibilities for action. It is proper to creatures to be limited in their being. Refusing to depend on the Creator is refusing to be what we are, and in so doing we risk ending up in self-destruction. On the other hand, it is wrong to understand dependence on God as alienation. Here again,

[15] Jean-Paul Sartre, *The Flies*, act III, pp. 116, 117, 119.

comparison with the child and his mother helps us understand. Consider the case of the child still in the mother's womb: the child is indeed totally dependent on its mother, but this dependence is not alienation; on the contrary, it is with love that the mother carries her child, and it is because of this dependence on its mother that the child can live and develop. It would be absurd to consider this dependence as an unacceptable alienation for the child. The situation is analogous to the level of creation, yet with this great difference: God and man are not on the same plane, since God infinitely transcends man. God is not a tyrant seeking to keep me forcibly in absolute dependence on him and make me his slave. By the act of creation, he carries me in being and gives me the gift of being who I am, a *person*. God does not create slaves, but persons who are truly able to be in a face-to-face encounter with him. Far from being the rival of human freedom, God is its source. Depending on God is therefore not alienation for man.

THE CREATOR'S PATERNITY

Moreover, this God on whom we depend is not some being at a distance from his creatures. He most certainly transcends them all, but his creative action makes him near to them, so that, in the lovely words of St. Augustine, God is more deeply within us than the deepest part of ourselves, and higher than highest part of ourselves: "*intimior intimo meo et superior summo meo.*"[16] Inwardness bespeaks the immanence of God, present to his creatures; height bespeaks his transcendence beyond all that exists.

We can further specify the relationship that unites us to God by saying that, by creation, God creates our spiritual soul within us. The act of creation does not directly con-

[16] St. Augustine, *The Confessions*, III.6.11, p. 63.

cern our bodies, but it does directly touch our souls. Our bodies come from our parents, while our souls do not come from our parents but come directly from God.[17] The Greek philosophers called the human intelligence "the divine part" of the soul, that by which man bears some resemblance to the gods and that which the gods most appreciate in man.[18] Some of them even spoke of a paternity of God for man. If God is the one who communicates to me my spiritual soul, the principle of my life of intelligence and love, then it is right to say that God is the father of my spirit. Cleanthes' "Hymn to Zeus" gives us an example of this acknowledgment of God as our father:

> *O God most glorious, called by many a name*
> *Nature's great King, through endless years the same;*
> *Omnipotence, who by thy just decree*
> *Controllest all, hail. . . .*
> *Zeus the all-bountiful, whom darkness shrouds,*
> *Whose lightning lightens the thunder-clouds,*
> *Thy children save from error's deadly sway:*
> *Turn thou the darkness from their souls away:*
> *Vouchsafe that unto knowledge they attain;*
> *For thou by knowledge art made strong to reign*
> *O'er all, and all things rule righteously.*[19]

[17] I do not mean that the human body is uncreated. Like every material reality, it is created by God. I do mean the following: the act of creation immediately bears on the spiritual soul. Our bodies come from pre-existing matter that was not created at the same time as our souls. It is bound up with the physical universe, which naturally depends on God in its existence. When a cat is generated, its "soul" (we can use this word by analogy to designate its immanent principle of life) is not created directly by God but comes from its progenitors. There is no new intervention by the Creator at the moment of the generation of a cat, but there is for the begetting of a man, for in this case God creates a new spiritual human soul. Aristotle had already understood that the human soul, in its intellective part (the intelligence), does not come from the parents, even though he does not explicitly affirm that it comes from God.

[18] See Aristotle, *Nicomachean Ethics* X.9. I cite a passage of this text on p. 26.

[19] Cleanthes, "Hymn to Zeus," in Jason L. Saunders, ed., *Greek and Roman Philosophy after Aristotle*. New York: The Free Press, 1966, pp. 149–150. Cleanthes was a Stoic philosopher of the fourth century B.C.

God's paternity of the soul is affirmed also by Plotinus:

> *How is it, then, that souls forget the divinity that begot them so that—divine by nature, divine by origin—they now know neither divinity nor self? . . . Once tasting the pleasures of independence, they use their freedom to go in a direction that leads away from their origin. And when they have gone a great distance, they even forget that they came from it.*[20]

THE CREATOR'S GAZE

It is important to understand the Creator's paternity of the persons he creates. In this light, we may speak of the Creator's gaze. How does the Creator look at me? Is it possible to adore God without knowing anything about how he considers me? Here again, we encounter various conceptions about the way God looks at man.

According to Voltaire, God indeed knows man but, deep down, man is indifferent to him, and vice versa. This is what Voltaire clearly expresses in the famous phrase: "God? We salute, but we do not speak."[21] In other words, God knows that man exists, and man knows that God exists, but they are indifferent to each other. They are like two individuals whose paths cross on the street from time to time and who make a polite gesture without ever opening their mouths.

For Sartre, on the contrary, the thought that God sees everything man does is completely unbearable. The following episode from his youth bears witness to this:

> *For several years more, I maintained public relations with the Almighty. But privately, I ceased to associate with Him. Only once did I have the feeling that He existed. I had been playing with*

[20] Plotinus, *Enneads*, V.1.1, p. 91.
[21] Voltaire, *Lettre à Piron.*

matches and burned a small rug. I was in the process of covering up my crime when suddenly God saw me. I felt His gaze inside my head and on my hands. I whirled about in the bathroom, horribly visible, a live target. Indignation saved me. I flew into a rage against so crude an indiscretion, I blasphemed, I muttered like my grandfather: "God damn it, God damn it, God damn it." He never looked at me again.[22]

In this text God's gaze is completely caricatured. God is nothing but a pitiless supervisor, a monitor constantly spying on man to reproach him for his sins. Any idea of a look of kindness from God is totally absent. We find something similar with Simone de Beauvoir:

To look at the world is, for [Fosca], to lay it waste, for he sees with the eye of God, whom I rejected at the age of fifteen, the eye of the Being who transcends and levels everything, who knows everything, who can do anything, and turns man into a worm. From everyone he encounters, Fosca steals the world, without reciprocity; he casts them into the agonizing indifference of eternity.[23]

Simone de Beauvoir conceives of God's gaze as something that crushes man to the point of reducing him to the state of a worm. If God does know everything, if he is all-powerful, there seems to be nothing left of man before him. We understand, then, how the instinctive reaction to reject God finally comes about.

Having rejected an inquisitorial idea of the divine gaze, and then God himself, Sartre is left with nothing but the void. This is what he expresses through the character Goetz in his play *The Devil and the Good Lord*:

Each minute I wondered what I could be in the eyes of God. Now I know the answer: nothing. God does not see me, God does not hear

[22] Jean-Paul Sartre, *Words*, I, p. 102.
[23] Simone de Beauvoir, *Force of Circumstance*, Volume 1, p. 65. Fosca is a character in her *All Men are Mortal*.

me, God does not know me. You see this emptiness over our heads? That is God. You see this gap in the door? It is God. You see that hole in the ground? That is God again. Silence is God. Absence is God. God is the loneliness of man. There was no one but myself; I alone decided on Evil; and I alone invented Good. It was I who cheated, I who worked miracles, I who accused myself today, I alone who can absolve myself; I, man. If God exists, man is nothing; if man exists . . .[24]

These misconceptions, even caricatures, of God's way of looking at humanity are interesting and make us understand the danger of anthropomorphism in speaking about God. Actually, God's gaze on man is totally different from what Sartre rejects. God certainly sees and knows each of his creatures intimately, but he looks on his spiritual creatures like a father full of kindness and love. God is not jealous of man; on the contrary, he is the one who communicates to him his soul, with its ability to know and love. He is the one who gives him the gift of being a person; being infinite goodness and the source of every good, he communicates to him his own personal goodness. Far from being the rival of human freedom, God is on the contrary the one who is its source. God is the one who loves man first, and his love is totally gratuitous and disinterested, since creation adds nothing to God's perfection. The Creator's love for man is therefore unique in its purity and clarity. Man's love for the one who is his creator and father is what this first love calls for in return; that is what adoration is in its natural dimension.

CONTEMPLATION OF GOD

If the Creator looks at man with so much love, man can also seek to "look at God," that is, to contemplate him.

---

[24] Jean-Paul Sartre, *The Devil and the Good Lord*, act III, scene 10, p. 141.

Of course, God is not immediately visible to man, and man only has knowledge of him analogically, mediated by the created realities in his experience. Limited and imperfect as it is, this contemplation of God is a profound desire of the human heart, even if this desire often remains buried by other desires. The Greek philosophers held contemplation in high regard. Some of them, such as Aristotle, have left us beautiful thoughts on contemplation of God:

> *We ought not to listen to those who warn us that "man should think the thoughts of man," or "mortal thoughts fit mortal minds"; but we ought, so far as in us lies, to put on immortality, and do all that we can do to live in conformity with the highest that is in us [that is, our intellect]. . . .*
>
> *Men have always conceived of [the gods] as at least living beings, and therefore active; for we cannot suppose that they spend their time in sleeping. . . . It follows, then, that the activity of God, which is supremely happy, must be a form of contemplation; and therefore among human activities that which is most akin to God's will be the happiest. . . . Thus happiness is a form of contemplation.*
>
> *The man who exercises his intellect and cultivates it seems likely to be in the best state of mind and to be most loved by the gods. For if, as is generally supposed, the gods have some concern for human affairs, it would be reasonable to believe also that they take pleasure in that part of us which is best and most closely related to themselves (this being the intellect), and that they reward those who appreciate and honor it most highly; for they care for what is dear to them, and what they do is right and good. Now it is not hard to see that it is the wise man that possesses these qualities in the highest degree; therefore he is dearest to the gods. And it is natural that he should also be the happiest of men. So on this score too the wise man will be happy in the highest degree.*[25]

---

[25] Aristotle, *Nicomachean Ethics*, X: 7 (1177b2–5), 8 (1178b18–32), 9 (1179a23–30), pp. 330–331, 333, 335.

Modern and contemporary philosophy has quite generally lost this sense of the nobility of contemplation, yet not totally. It seems that an aspiration to contemplation of God is found in Heidegger, even though he himself does not put it in these terms. One may wonder whether "thinking Being," which for Heidegger is the highest and noblest human task, is to him a sort of substitute for contemplation of God. Perhaps we could say something analogous, but in an entirely different way, of Levinas, for whom contemplation of the face of the other holds such great importance. The evolution of modern philosophy since Kant[26] has made elaboration of philosophical wisdom most difficult for the contemporary period, but it is interesting to notice in some thinkers a kind of appeal, tenuous though it may be, toward transcendence.

RELIGIOUS ETHICS

The act of adoration is the basis of a particular dimension of the human person, the religious dimension. Philosophical study of man as a religious being permits the development of religious ethics. Religious ethics presupposes human ethics; it is a new development for human ethics in the light of the existence of the Creator. It is concerned with the different acts by which man freely responds to his creation by the Creator: adoration, contemplation, prayer, sacrifices, liturgy, and so on.[27] This human reli-

---

[26] Kant (1724–1804) was the first philosopher to say that it was impossible for human intelligence to reach the existence of God, and on this point he was a considerable influence on later philosophers, and even some theologians. Kant saw this impossibility positively: for him, the abolition of any philosophical knowledge of God would allow the entire place once occupied by this knowledge to be left to faith. In reality, it deprives the religious attitude of its natural foundation.

[27] For a philosophical study of liturgy, see: Samuel Rouvillois, *Corps et sagesse: Philosophie de la liturgie.*

gious activity is regulated by a particular human virtue, the virtue of religion. The human religious attitude needs to be educated. The virtue of religion enables man to carry out religious activity in conformity with reason, without letting himself be carried away by passion, as unfortunately happens in religious fanaticism. Man's religious activity, and adoration in particular, needs to be purified and rectified. Perfectly pure adoration of the Creator is not something to which one comes immediately. However, although religious fanaticism is a perversion of the religious attitude to which our era, especially in the West, is particularly sensitive, atheism and religious indifference are not good either; they are vices "by defect," whereas fanaticism is a vice "by excess." Creation is part of the truth about man. Denying the existence of the Creator or practically living as though he did not exist does not correspond to the truth about the human person. This denial would prevent the flowering of man's authentic religious dimension and would risk mutilating him. It is therefore important to have an authentic religious education, one which includes the progressive acquisition of the virtue of religion. From this point of view, learning to adore the Creator is something essential, inasmuch as adoration is the fundamental religious act. An authentic religious education must teach adoration of God and, at the same time, respect for each human person, because each person bears a resemblance to the Creator at the level of his or her spirit. It is regrettable that the religious education of children and young adults is so often deficient on this point, sometimes even among Christians.

There is much more to say about adoration on the philosophical plane,[28] but our purpose here was essentially

---

[28] On this point, also see: Marie-Dominique Goutierre, *L'Homme face à sa mort. L'absurde ou le salut?*

to make clear that adoration is a fundamental human act. We see that, although it is necessary to know the existence of the Creator (or to believe in his existence by religious tradition) in order to speak of adoration, it is not necessary to appeal to Christian faith in order to speak of it, since adoration has a natural foundation. We can speak of the importance of adoration today in encounters with Muslims, for they have a developed sense of adoration. Seeing the place adoration takes in their lives, they often seem to know adoration better than many Christians! There is something beautiful about seeing Muslims, unfazed by other people's opinions, make their prostrations on the ground at the hour of prayer to adore God. In saying this, I do not mean that the adoration of Muslims is the same as the adoration of Christians—we shall see that this is not the case—but I do mean to say that their adoration has a natural foundation.[29] Adoration is an important meeting point between Muslims and Christians in interreligious dialogue.[30] Could the growing number of Muslims in Europe be an opportunity for many Christians to rediscover the importance of adoration in human life? This must be our wish.

[29] On adoration in Islam, see: Jacques Jomier, "L'Adoration dans le monde musulman," *Aletheia: L'Adoration* 12, pp. 99–107; Mamady Alkaly Chérif, "Prière et adoration en islam," ibid., pp. 109–114.

[30] It does seem that, beyond the Judeo-Christian world, Islam has the most developed sense of adoration.

Chapter 2: Adoration in the Old Testament

After a quick philosophical reflection on adoration as an act of natural human love for the Creator, it is time to turn to Sacred Scripture to see what the Bible has to say about adoration. We begin with the Old Testament. This will not be a detailed study of adoration in the Old Testament, but will focus on a few of its most important aspects.[31]

THE OLD TESTAMENT VOCABULARY OF ADORATION

The Hebrew mentality is very concrete and much less given to speculation than the Greek. For this reason, adoration in the Old Testament does not first mean a spiritual act but rather a concrete gesture, that of prostrating oneself before God, an act which the Hebrew text usually expresses with the verb *hishtachawah*. The first occurrence of this verb is found in the episode of the Lord's appearance to Abraham at Mamre, when Abraham bows down before the Lord, who manifests himself to him (Gen 18:2).

We must observe, however, that the gesture of prostration is not reserved to God in the Old Testament. In many cases, we see Jews prostrate themselves before a man: Jacob before Esau (Gen 33:3-7); the sons of Jacob before Joseph (Gen 37:9; 42:6; 43:26); David before Saul (1 Sam 24:9); Bathsheba and Nathan before David (1 Kgs 1:16);

---

[31] On adoration in the Old Testament, see in particular: Marie-Jérôme Ternynck, *"L'Adoration dans la Bible."*

Solomon before Bathsheba (1 Kgs 2:19) and Ruth before Boaz (Ruth 2:10). Here, prostration is clearly a mark of honor toward a person by reason of his or her eminent position. We must wait until nearly the end of the Old Testament, with the book of Esther, to see a Jew refuse to prostrate himself before another man (Mordechai before Haman, cf. Esther 3:2); this is an evolution that reaches its completion in the New Testament, in which Jesus alone is so honored, as we shall see.

THE SACRIFICES OF THE OLD COVENANT [32]

In the Old Testament, adoration is also concretized by offering to God a sacrifice or even by the erection of an altar. We see this at the beginning of Genesis, with the sacrifices of Cain and Abel, the sacrifice of Noah, and the sacrifices offered by the patriarchs.[33] The connection between sacrifice and adoration is made by Abraham in Genesis 22:5: "Abraham said to his young men, 'Stay here with the donkey; I and the lad will go yonder and worship, and come again to you.'"

One of the specific characteristics of this form of worship is that, unlike the pagan worship of the neighboring countries, it does not depend on the land in which the patriarch is located:

> *If Abraham does not adore the local divinity, if he does not go to the local shrine to curry the favor of that country's protector god, it is because Yahweh surpasses in universality and power the other particular divinities.*[34]

---

[32] A theological study of the various sacrifices offered to God under the Old Covenant may be found in *You Shall Worship One God* by Marie-Dominique Philippe.

[33] See Gen 4:3–5; 8:20; 12:7–8; 13:18; 22:9; 26:25; 33:20; 35:1,7.

[34] Marie-Jérôme Ternynck, "*L'Adoration dans la Bible*," p. 14.

This informal worship of God will later become worship organized by the Law of Moses, which will give a whole body of legislation concerning the Levitical priesthood and the various types of sacrifices the Hebrews may offer to God.

THE FIRST COMMANDMENT OF THE LAW

After their departure from Egypt, the people of Israel, under the guidance of Moses, arrive at the mountain of Sinai, where God enters into a covenant with them, making them his people, a holy people. The covenant of Sinai involves the gift to Israel of a law, which we commonly call "the Law of Moses," and even simply "the Law." This Law includes an extreme diversity of precepts, which can be classified into three main groups:
— moral precepts, meant to regulate the moral life of Israel;
— cultic precepts, specifying all the legislation of the priesthood, worship, and sacrifices to God;
— juridical precepts, meant to organize the social life of Israel as a people.

The presentation of these precepts is found in the three great sets of legislation in the Pentateuch, which are called the Covenant Code (Ex 21-23), the Deuteronomic Code (Dt 12-26), and the Law of Holiness (Lv 17-26).

In Exodus, the Covenant Code is immediately preceded by the Decalogue (the "Ten Words" or "Ten Commandments"), which contains the nucleus of the moral precepts of the Law of Moses. This is how the Decalogue begins:[35]

I am the Lord your God, who brought you out of the land of Egypt, out of the house of bondage.

[35] The Book of Deuteronomy gives another version of the Decalogue at Dt 5:6–21.

You shall have no other gods before me.
You shall not make for yourself a graven image, or any likeness of anything that is in Heaven above, or that is in the earth beneath, or that is in the water under the earth; you shall not bow down to them or serve them; for I the Lord your God am a jealous God, visiting the iniquity of the fathers upon the children to the third and the fourth generation of those who hate me.[36]

It is significant that the first commandment of the Decalogue has to do with adoration. This commandment is expressed in a negative mode of prohibition: the Hebrews must not adore (that is, prostrate themselves before) gods other than Yahweh. But this prohibition is the negative side of a positive precept found in Deuteronomy, the *Shema Israel* ("Hear, O Israel"), the great precept of love for God:

> *Hear, O Israel: the Lord our God is one Lord; and you shall love the Lord your God with all your heart, and with all your soul, and with all your might. And these words which I command you this day shall be upon your heart.*[37]

Adoring God is loving him with all one's heart and soul, offering him a faithful love, one not offered to others, but set apart for him alone. The two precepts of Exodus 20:5 and Deuteronomy 6:5 therefore constitute a profound unity. In the New Covenant, Christ will manifest this unity in his answer to the Devil who invites Jesus to adore him:

> *It is written, "You shall worship the Lord your God and him only shall you serve."*[38]

---

[36] Ex 20:2–5. The prohibition against bowing down before other gods is repeated in Ex 23:24.
[37] Dt 6:4–6.
[38] Mt 4:10.

We saw in the philosophical part that adoration has a natural foundation and that man has within him a natural aspiration to adore God. If this is indeed the case, we might wonder what need there is to make adoration into a precept. Do people need this? St. Augustine gives us a deep insight on this point when he says that God engraved on the tablets of stone the precepts man could no longer read on the little tablet of his heart.[39] This holds true for all the precepts of the Law and in particular for the precept of love for God. In other words, it is because man after original sin had great difficulty understanding how important adoration was for him.[40]

THE TEMPTATION OF IDOLATRY

We find ample confirmation of this difficulty in the history of Israel. Even in the time of the patriarchs, Rachel, Jacob's wife, stole her father Laban's domestic idols (Genesis 31:19). After the patriarchs, it is striking to see how much trouble the people of Israel have remaining faithful to the precept of adoring Yahweh. The Old Testament shows us how this people is constantly tempted to adore idols. According to the Book of Exodus, the temptation came very quickly, with the episode of the golden calf:

> *When the people saw that Moses delayed to come down from the mountain, the people gathered themselves together to Aaron, and said to him, "Up, make us gods, who shall go before us; as for this*

[39] St. Augustine, *Commentary on the Psalms*, 57.1. This explanation is taken up by St. Bonaventure: "A full explanation of the commandments of the Decalogue became necessary in the state of sin because the light of reason was obscured and the will had gone astray" (quoted in the *Catechism of the Catholic Church* at 2071).

[40] It is the same for all the precepts of the Decalogue. According to St. Thomas Aquinas, they pertain to natural law, yet it was good for them to be prescribed to Israel.

Moses, the man who brought us up out of the land of Egypt, we do not know what has become of him. " *And Aaron said to them, "Take off the rings of gold which are in the ears of your wives, your sons, and your daughters, and bring them to me.* " *So all the people took off the rings of gold which were in their ears, and brought them to Aaron. And he received the gold at their hand, and fashioned it with a graving tool, and made a molten calf; and they said, "These are your gods, O Israel, who brought you up out of the land of Egypt!" When Aaron saw this, he built an altar before it; and Aaron made proclamation and said, "Tomorrow shall be a feast to the Lord.* " [41]

We often think that Israel's sin consisted in forsaking Yahweh for another god, symbolized by the golden calf. However, we should be more precise: in the strict sense, the Hebrews had no intention of changing divinities, since Aaron himself declared a feast day for Yahweh, and therefore for the God of Israel. This shows that he did not consider the golden calf to be the representation of a different god. The nature of the Hebrews' sin was rather a total lack of respect for God's transcendence by lowering Yahweh to the sensible level. Joseph Ratzinger explains this well:

The cult conducted by the high priest Aaron is not meant to serve any of the false gods of the heathen. The apostasy is more subtle. There is not obvious turning away from God to the false gods. Outwardly, the people remain completely attached to the same God. They want to glorify the God who led Israel out of Egypt and believe that they may very properly represent his mysterious power in the image of a bull calf. Everything seems to be in order. Presumably even the ritual is in complete conformity to the rubrics. And yet it is a falling away from the worship of God to idolatry. This apostasy, which outwardly is scarcely perceptible, has two causes. First, there is a violation of the prohibition of images. The people cannot cope with the invisible, remote, and mysterious God. They want to bring him down into their own world, into what they

[41] Ex 32:1–5.

can see and understand. Worship is no longer going up to God, but drawing God down into one's own world. He must be there when he is needed, and he must be the kind of God that is needed. Man is using God, and in reality, even if it is not outwardly discernible, he is placing himself above God. This gives us a clue to the second point. The worship of the golden calf is a self-generated cult. When Moses stays away for too long, and God himself becomes inaccessible, the people just fetch him back. Worship becomes a feast that the community gives itself, a festival of self-affirmation. Instead of being worship of God, it becomes a circle closed in on itself: eating, drinking, and making merry. The dance around the golden calf is an image of this self-seeking worship. It is a kind of banal self-gratification.[42]

The Lord pointed out this very sin to Moses, when he was still on the mountain with him:

Go down; for your people, whom you brought up out of the land of Egypt, have corrupted themselves; they have turned aside quickly out of the way which I commanded them; they have made for themselves a molten calf, and have worshiped it and sacrificed to it, and said, 'These are your gods, O Israel, who brought you up out of the land of Egypt!'[43]

Even while having mercy on his people by not destroying them, thanks to the intercession of Moses, God still severely punished those at fault.

Once they were established in the Promised Land, the people of Israel kept being tempted to idolatry. The beginning of the book of Judges shows us Israel adoring the neighboring peoples' divinities, thus arousing the wrath of Yahweh:

And the sons of Israel did what was evil in the sight of the Lord and served the Baals; and they forsook the Lord, the God of their fathers, who had brought them out of the land of Egypt; they went

[42] Joseph Ratzinger, *The Spirit of the Liturgy*, pp. 22–23.
[43] Ex 32:7–8.

after other gods, from among the gods of the peoples who were round about them, and bowed down to them; and they provoked the Lord to anger. They forsook the Lord, and served the Baals and the Ashtaroth. So the anger of the Lord was kindled against Israel, and he gave them over to plunderers, who plundered them; and he sold them into the power of their enemies round about, so that they could no longer withstand their enemies. Whenever they marched out, the hand of the Lord was against them for evil, as the Lord had warned, and as the Lord had sworn to them; and they were in great distress.[44]

We must understand the meaning of this divine wrath, which the Bible sometimes calls "jealousy," as an anthropomorphic expression. It is a strong way to signify that God is not indifferent to man's attitude toward him. God also knows that it is man's good to adore the true God and that idolatry harms the human heart. Finally, it is important to bear in mind that God had entrusted a special mission to Israel: in the midst of the neighboring peoples of the Near East, who were all polytheistic, Israel was to take care to keep faith and adoration toward the one God, the Creator of the universe, and it was to give witness of this faith and adoration to the other peoples. Israel's religious infidelity therefore also had negative consequences for the other peoples, who were deprived of this witness.

In this regard, Israel's kings had a particular responsibility. It was up to them not only to give the example but also to watch over the people's fidelity to the covenant and therefore to adoration. Whatever their personal weaknesses, the first two kings of Israel, Saul and especially David, remained faithful to monotheism. Unfortunately, King Solomon, in his old age, authorized his pagan wives to set up shrines to their divinities out of weakness:

---

[44] Judg 2:11–15.

When Solomon was old his wives turned away his heart after other gods; and his heart was not wholly true to the Lord his God, as was the heart of David his father. For Solomon went after Ashtoreth the goddess of the Sidonians, and after Milcom the abomination of the Ammonites. So Solomon did what was evil in the sight of the Lord, and did not wholly follow the Lord, as David his father had done. Then Solomon built a high place for Chemosh the abomination of Moab, and for Molech the abomination of the Ammonites, on the mountain east of Jerusalem. And so he did for all his foreign wives, who burned incense and sacrificed to their gods.[45]

This was a grave sin on his part, and it was punished by God in the form of the division of the kingdom of Solomon into two parts, the northern kingdom or kingdom of Israel and the southern kingdom or that of Judah, during the reign of Rehoboam, Solomon's son (cf. 1 Kgs 11-12). After this, the books of Kings show us that most of Israel and Judah's kings compromised with idolatry to varying degrees. Jeroboam, for example, the king of Israel after the schism, made two golden calves and sent them to Bethel. It is significant that the words he pronounced at that time were the same as Aaron's at the time of the casting of the golden calf during the exodus: "Behold your gods, O Israel, who brought you up out of the land of Egypt."[46] So God sent prophets to warn and correct his people, but they were hardly listened to, as we see in the cases of Elijah and Jeremiah. The famous episode of the sacrifice on Mount Carmel (1 Kgs 18) is centered on the problem of adoration: who is the true God worthy to be adored? Is it Yahweh, the God of Israel, or the Baals, the pagan divinities? The Israelites made compromises between the two, but Elijah told them that they had to choose:

[45] 1 Kgs 11:4–8. This passage makes us understand the prohibition in the Law of Moses against marrying a foreign woman (see Dt 7:1–4); the risk of contamination of faith in Yahweh was very real.
[46] 1 Kgs 12:28. See 12:26–33.

So Ahab sent to all the people of Israel, and gathered the prophets together at Mount Carmel. And Elijah came near to all the people, and said, "How long will you go limping with two different opinions? If the Lord is God, follow him; but if Baal, then follow him." And the people did not answer him a word.[47]

Faced with the embarassed silence of the people, aware of its religious syncretism, Elijah proposed a sort of contest with the prophets of Baal: each side was to offer a sacrifice to its god, they to Baal, Elijah to Yahweh; the god who answered with fire was the one who is God. And Elijah won this contest:

And at the time of the offering of the oblation, Elijah the prophet came near and said, "O Lord, God of Abraham, Isaac, and Israel, let it be known this day that you are God in Israel, and that I am your servant, and that I have done all these things at your word. Answer me, O Lord, answer me, that this people may know that you, O Lord, are God, and that you have turned their hearts back." Then the fire of the Lord fell, and consumed the burnt offering, and the wood, and the stones, and the dust, and licked up the water that was in the trench. And when all the people saw it, they fell on their faces; and they said, "The Lord, he is God; the Lord, he is God."[48]

In his mercy for Israel, unfaithful to the covenant, God sent them the prophet Elijah to remind them of the importance of faithfulness to adoration of the one God. He gave Elijah the working of prodigious signs to strike the Israelites with astonishment and touch their hearts.

Unfortunately, this renewal in the days of Elijah seems to have been short-lived. The Israelites returned to their religious and moral infidelities. These grave religious infidelities, and many other sins besides, caused the chastisement of the destruction of the Jerusalem Temple by the

[47] 1 Kgs 18:20–21.
[48] 1 Kgs 18:36–39.

Chaldeans in 587 B.C. Deportation was not only a chastisement, but also an opportunity for Israel's profound purification. Exiled to Babylon, the Jews had plenty of time to
meditate on the causes of the disaster they had undergone.
The Spirit of the Lord worked in their hearts and aroused
the desire to return, not only to the Holy Land, but still
more deeply to come back to the Lord and to be more
faithful from then on.

In the second century B.C., Israel had to face an especially fearsome trial when Antiochus Epiphanes, the king
of Syria who reigned over the region, decided to force the
Jews to renounce their religion:

> *The king wrote to his whole kingdom that all should be one people,*
> *and that each should give up his customs. All the Gentiles accepted*
> *the command of the king. Many even from Israel gladly adopted*
> *his religion; they sacrificed to idols and profaned the Sabbath. And*
> *the king sent letters by messengers to Jerusalem and the cities of*
> *Judah; he directed them to follow customs strange to the land, to*
> *forbid burnt offerings and sacrifices and drink offerings in the*
> *sanctuary, to profane sabbaths and feasts, to defile the sanctuary*
> *and the priests, to build altars and sacred precincts and shrines for*
> *idols, to sacrifice swine and unclean animals, and to leave their sons*
> *uncircumcised. They were to make themselves abominable by*
> *everything unclean and profane, so that they should forget the law*
> *and change all the ordinances. "And whoever does not obey the*
> *command of the king shall die."* [49]

Many Jews submitted to the king's decree, but others
preferred to resist to the point of shedding their blood,
if necessary, to remain faithful to the covenant with
Yahweh, the God of Israel. This was the Maccabean revolt. One particularly moving episode from this revolt
was the martyrdom of a mother's seven sons, recounted in
detail in 2 Maccabees 7. Ordered to eat pork—something

---

[49] 1 Mac 1:41–50.

forbidden by the Law of Moses—the seven brothers refused, preferring death. After the death of the first two, the third brother declared, "I got these [hands and tongue] from Heaven, and because of his laws I disdain them, and from him I hope to get them back again" (2 Mac 7:11). He therefore acknowledged receiving his human life from the Creator and reckoned faithfulness to his covenant to be worth more than his own life. Theologically, the mother's last exhortations to her sons are especially important:

> *I do not know how you came into being in my womb. It was not I who gave you life and breath, nor I who set in order the elements within each of you. Therefore the Creator of the world, who shaped the beginning of man and devised the origin of all things, will in his mercy give life and breath back to you again, since you now forget yourselves for the sake of his laws. . . .*
> *My son, have pity on me. I carried you nine months in my womb, and nursed you for three years, and have reared you and brought you up to this point in your life, and have taken care of you. I beseech you, my child, to look at the Heaven and the earth and see everything that is in them, and recognize that God did not make them out of things that existed. Thus also mankind comes into being. Do not fear this butcher.*[50]

This admirable mother recognized that the Creator, not she, was the first origin of her children's life and spirit. He was the one who created the universe "not out of things that existed." It is amazing to see the context in which this important affirmation about creation first appears in Scripture. At the beginning of Genesis, it is said, "In the beginning God created the Heavens and earth" (Gen 1:1), but the sacred author does not specify whether or not God created the world from pre-existing matter.[51] In the context of bloody martyrdom, near the end of the

---

[50] 2 Mac 7:22–23; 27–29.

[51] In Plato's *Timaeus*, the demiurge is said to have formed the universe from pre-existing matter.

Old Testament, this most important assertion springs from the mouth of a mother. If God is able to raise up human beings from nothing, then he is just as able to raise them up again after death.

So we see just how difficult fidelity to adoration of the one God was for Israel. The difficulties came both from the Jews' weakness (as in the episode of the golden calf) and from the influence, and even coercion, of neighboring peoples. Even soldiers of Judas Maccabeus' own army gave in to temptation by wearing objects consecrated to idols (2 Mac 12:40).

THE ONENESS OF GOD

Progressively, Israel came to the clear awareness of God's oneness. In this theological progression, several stages may be discerned.

Abraham received the order to leave his homeland to follow God's call and be bound exclusively to him (Gen 12). When he left his country, he also had to abandon the local divinities he had previously honored.[52] Yahweh became his God and remained so everywhere Abraham lived in the course of his travels.

With the Law of Moses, the Hebrews received the strict prohibition against adoring other gods, yet we observe that the Decalogue does not assert that the pagans' gods are nothing at all.

It is essentially with Deutero-Isaiah (Is 40-55), in the period of the return from exile in Babylon (sixth century B.C.), that awareness of God's oneness clearly and explicitly appears. Yahweh, the God of Israel, is the one God, and there is no other:

---

[52] *The Apocalypse of Abraham*, a non-canonical Jewish text written between 70 and 150 A.D., claims that before his calling by God, Abraham argued against his father Terah's idols. This is an anachronistic projection onto the past.

Thus says the Lord, the King of Israel and his Redeemer, the Lord of hosts: "I am the first and I am the last; besides me there is no god. Who is like me? Let him proclaim it, let him declare and set it forth before me.

I am the Lord, and there is no other, besides me there is no God.[53]

Until this time, idolatry was rejected with horror by the Jews faithful to the covenant. After this time, the rejection of idolatry was often accompanied by biting critiques of the pagans' idolatry, especially the fabrication of idols. We find examples of this later attitude in certain Psalms (Ps 115[113B], Ps 135[134]) and at the end of the Old Testament in the Book of Wisdom, which contains a polemic against the pagans' idolatry, reproaching them for having been unable to discover the one God (Wis 13).

GOD'S GAZE IN THE OLD COVENANT

Our philosophical reflection on adoration in the previous chapter considered the Creator's way of looking at his human creatures in order to understand that his look is one of benevolent love. Let us look at a few passages of the Old Testament on this subject:

The Lord looks down from Heaven, he sees all the sons of men; from where he sits enthroned he looks forth on all the inhabitants of the earth, he who fashions the hearts of them all, and observes all their deeds.

Behold, the eye of the Lord is on those who fear him, on those who hope in his steadfast love, that he may deliver their souls from death, and keep them alive in famine.[54]

For it is always in your power to show great strength, and who can withstand the might of your arm? Because the whole world before

---
[53] Is 44:6–7; 45:5.
[54] Ps 33(32):13–15, 18–19.

you is like a speck that tips the scales, and like a drop of morning dew that falls upon the ground. But you are merciful to all, for you can do all things, and you overlook men's sins, that they may repent. For you love all things that exist, and have loathing for none of the things which you have made, for you would not have made anything if you had hated it. How would anything have endured if you had not willed it? Or how would anything not called forth by you have been preserved? You spare all things, for they are yours, O Lord who love the living. For your immortal spirit is in all things.[55]

We are far indeed from the surveillance of the policeman–god imagined by Sartre. Of course, Scripture does affirm God's intimate knowledge of human acts but also that his look on human beings is one of love and mercy.

As one who knows that God looks at him with kindness, the Psalmist assiduously seeks the Lord's face:

Hear, O Lord, when I cry aloud, be gracious to me and answer me! You have said, "Seek my face." My heart says to you, "Your face, Lord, do I seek." Hide not your face from me.[56]

O God, you are my God, I seek you, my soul thirsts for you; my flesh faints for you, as in a dry and weary land where no water is. So I have looked upon you in the sanctuary, beholding your power and glory.[57]

Many psalms exhort to the adoration of God:

For the Lord is a great God, and a great King above all gods. In his hand are the depths of the earth; the heights of the mountains are his also. The sea is his, for he made it; for his hands formed the dry land. O come, let us worship and bow down, let us kneel before the Lord, our Maker! For he is our God, and we are the people of his pasture, and the sheep of his hand.[58]

---

[55] Wis 11:21–12:1.   [56] Ps 27(26):7–9.   [57] Ps 63(62):1–2.
[58] Ps 95(94):3–7. It is significant that the Christian Liturgy of the Hours begins each day with this psalm, which shows how adoration is fundamental to Christian prayer.

Extol the Lord our God; worship at his footstool! Holy is he!
　Extol the Lord our God, and worship at his holy mountain; for
the Lord our God is holy! [59]

To conclude our look at the Old Testament, we can say that adoration constituted at once the primary demand for Israel in its covenant with God and its fundamental religious education.

[59] Ps 99(98):5, 9.

Chapter 3: Adoration in the New Testament

As we approach the New Testament, we must call to mind what Jesus says in the Sermon on the Mount:

> *Think not that I have come to abolish the law and the prophets; I have come not to abolish them but to fulfill them. For truly, I say to you, till Heaven and earth pass away, not an iota, not a dot, will pass from the law until all is accomplished.*[60]

Jesus does not come to do away with the Law of Moses but to bring it to perfection.[61] This is also the case for the precept of adoration, the first precept of the Law of Moses. We may therefore expect to see Jesus bring the adoration of the Old Testament to perfection.

However, before looking at some of the great New Testament passages on adoration, it would be appropriate to say a few words about the vocabulary for adoration in the New Testament.

ADORATION VOCABULARY IN THE NEW TESTAMENT

The Greek word most often translated as "worship" or "adore" in English versions of the New Testament is the

---

[60] Mt 5:17–18.

[61] St. Matthew shows this so well in his Gospel by the antitheses at the beginning of the Sermon on the Mount (Mt 5:20–48), in which Jesus cites a precept of the Decalogue and then gives his own prescription: "You have heard that it was said . . . But I say to you . . .".

verb *proskuneō,* so it is important for us to know the meaning of this verb.[62]

The etymology of the verb *proskuneō* is obscure. According to the most commonly held opinion, *proskuneō* is composed of the preposition *pros* (toward) and the verb *kuneō,* meaning "to kiss." Literally, then, *proskuneō* means "to send a kiss to."[63] From the fifth century B.C., however, Herodotus and Euripides use the noun *proskunēsis* (or hereafter "proskynesis") to designate prostration followed by kissing the sovereign's feet in Persian court ceremonial.[64] In the Hellenistic world, the Greeks sent kisses to the gods' statues as an act of homage.[65] The proskynesis was often joined to a prostration of the body, and eventually came to designate the act of prostration. The Greeks reserved this gesture for their gods and were shocked by the "barbarous" eastern custom of giving homage to a man by prostrating before him.[66] Among the eastern peoples, however, this gesture did not imply recognition of divinity as such but was simply a way of giving solemn homage. It is important to keep in mind that the concept and practice of proskynesis was different for Greeks and Orientals.

---

[62] Here I bring in elements of a more in-depth study, *"L'Adoration dans l'Apocalypse,"* published in *Chemins à travers l'Apocalypse,* p. 63–148. For more information on the verb *proskuneo,* see the technical article on this subject by Heinrich Greeven in the *Theological Dictionary of the New Testament,* VI.

[63] On the other hand, many philologists maintain that the Latin verb *adorare* (the origin of the English word "adore") has nothing to do with Latin *os* (mouth), contrary to a widely held belief; rather, it comes from the verb *orare,* "to speak" or "to pray" (see Oscar Bloch, *Dictionnaire de la langue française,* Paris: PUF 1950). Joseph Ratzinger disagrees with them, as we shall see later on.

[64] The ruler was considered a son of the god.

[65] The Jews never performed this gesture because of the proscription of representations of God in the Law of Moses.

[66] History recalls the episode of Bactria (327 B.C.), in which the Greeks refused to submit to the order of Alexander the Great to give him proskynesis.

However, as the Roman Empire expanded to the eastern provinces, the custom of giving the proskynesis to the Roman emperors developed.[67]

In the Septuagint (the Greek translation of the Old Testament), *proskuneō* is nearly the only translation of the words *hishtachawah* and *sagad*, which mean the act of bowing. In three quarters of the cases, it is used to mean the veneration and adoration of God or the false gods.

The verb *proskuneō* appears sixty times in the New Testament, twenty-nine of these being found in the Gospels and twenty-four in the Book of Revelation, which is by far the New Testament book that uses this verb the most.

The Gospel of Matthew uses *proskuneō* thirteen times. We see the proskynesis performed several times before Jesus: by the Magi (Mt 2:11), the leper (Mt 8:2), Jairus (Mt 9:18), the disciples in the boat (Mt 14:33), the Canaanite woman (Mt 15:25), and the mother of James and John (Mt 20:20).

The Gospel of Mark uses *proskuneō* only twice. The first time concerns the Roman soldiers mockingly bowing before Jesus during his Passion in Mark 15:19. The other time (Mk 5:6) has to do with the Gerasene demoniac who comes to meet Jesus and bows before him, crying out loudly, "What have you to do with me, Jesus, Son of the Most High God? I adjure you by God, do not torment me." This is the only New Testament text in which a demoniac gives Jesus the proskynesis. When we recall how the possessed knew Jesus (see Mk 1:24, 34) and the importance of the theme of confession of Jesus as the Son of God in Mark's Gospel (see Mk 1:1; 15:39), we are inclined to interpret this proskynesis as adoration, with the difference that here it is not an act of love but an act of forced homage.

---

[67] It seems that the first Roman emperor to have demanded the proskynesis was Caligula, who reigned from 37 to 41 A.D.

Luke, on the other hand, coming from and writing for a Hellenistic milieu, uses the verb *proskuneō* much more restrictively than Matthew, only twice and significantly. The first time, during the account of the temptation in the wilderness, it is to reject the Devil's pretention in calling on Jesus to adore him and to recall that adoration is reserved for God alone (Lk 4:7-8). The second time is at the moment of Christ's Ascension and is the only time in the third Gospel we see people—here, the disciples— give Jesus the proskynesis. The disciples' proskynesis before the risen Christ is likely adoration of Christ recognized as God.

The Fourth Gospel uses *proskuneō* eleven times. In John 12:20, the ones who perform this action are Greeks who have come up to Jerusalem, probably proselytes or at least sympathizers with the religion of Israel. The proskynesis of John 9:38 is that of the man born blind healed by Jesus who bows down before him. If we take the context into account, we may interpret this proskynesis as authentic adoration, inasmuch as the evangelist shows us the man born blind growing in faith to the point of being able to confess the Son of Man and to bow down before him. The most important passage of the Fourth Gospel about proskynesis, however, is unquestionably Jesus' conversation with the Samaritan woman (Jn 4), with nine uses of *proskuneō*. Because of its importance for adoration, we will study this passage later in greater detail.

Lastly, we must note that the verb *proskuneō* is seldom employed in the New Testament outside of the Gospels and Revelation. We find it only in Acts 7:43 (Stephen's address); Acts 8:27 (the Ethiopian eunuch in pilgrimage to Jerusalem); Acts 10:25 (Cornelius wanting to bow down before Peter); Acts 24:11; 1 Corinthians 14:25; Hebrews 1:6 and 11:21. Unquestionably, the Gospel of John and the Book of Revelation use this word most often.

THE CLEANSING OF THE TEMPLE (JOHN 2)

Among the Gospels, it is surely the fourth that best shows the importance of adoration in Jesus' eyes. This is seen in two places of this Gospel: the cleansing of the Temple (Jn 2:13-22) and the conversation with the Samaritan woman (Jn 4:1-42). We will first look at John 2.

Observe at the outset the situation of this episode in the Gospel of John: at the start of Jesus' apostolic life, after the wedding feast of Cana. The episode is also reported by the Synoptic Gospels, but we see it at the end of Jesus' apostolic life, shortly before the Passion. Exegetes argue over the dating of this action by Christ: Did it take place at the beginning or end of Jesus' ministry? We can argue this question historically,[68] but in any case we must understand the theological importance John gives this episode by reporting it at the beginning of Jesus' apostolic life. The way Jesus begins his apostolic life after his baptism in the Jordan is different in the four Gospels and reveals the particular theology of each of them.

In the Gospel of Mark, the evangelist presents us with a typical day of Christ's apostolate (Mk 1:21-39): Jesus preaches in the Capernaum synagogue, casts a demon out of a possessed person, heals some sick people, and ends his day with prayer.

---

[68] We must consider the fact that the Synoptic Gospels present Jesus' apostolic life such that it begins in Galilee and ends with (only) one ascent by Christ to Jerusalem for the Passion. In such a scheme, whose origin might be catechetical in nature, it is clear that the purification of the Temple can be placed only at the end of Jesus' life. Historically, an early dating, one at the beginning of Christ's apostolic life, seems more plausible to us than a late dating, inasmuch as it was more difficult for Jesus to perform this gesture at the end of his life, when his preaching had aroused such hostility among the Jewish authorities. We can also see how the Gospel of John is usually more historically precise than the Synoptic Gospels.

In Matthew's Gospel, Jesus begins his apostolate with the masterful Sermon on the Mount (Mt 5-7). In this way, Matthew suggests that Jesus is the new Moses who comes to complete and perfect the Law.

In Luke's Gospel, Jesus starts with a sermon in the Nazareth synagogue: "The Spirit of the Lord is upon me, because he has anointed me to preach good news to the poor. He has sent me . . . to proclaim the acceptable year of the Lord" (Lk 4:16-30). This preaching casts a valuable light on Jesus' apostolic life in Luke: Jesus comes to preach a year of grace, particularly for the poor.

Finally, in John's Gospel, Jesus begins his apostolic life with the wedding feast of Cana, thus presenting himself as the bridegroom of the messianic wedding feast. After a brief mention of passing through Capernaum, John presents Jesus going up to Jerusalem. In the Fourth Gospel, this is the first time Jesus goes up to Jerusalem. What is the purpose of his journey? He comes to cleanse the Temple:

The Passover of the Jews was at hand, and Jesus went up to Jerusalem. In the temple he found those who were selling oxen and sheep and pigeons, and the money-changers at their business. And making a whip of cords, he drove them all, with the sheep and oxen, out of the temple; and he poured out the coins of the money-changers and overturned their tables. And he told those who sold the pigeons, "Take these things away; you shall not make my Father's house a house of trade." His disciples remembered that it was written, "Zeal for your house will consume me." The Jews then said to him, "What sign have you to show us for doing this?" Jesus answered them, "Destroy this temple, and in three days I will raise it up." The Jews then said, "It has taken forty-six years to build this temple, and will you raise it up in three days?" But he spoke of the temple of his body. When therefore he was raised from the dead, his disciples remembered that he had said this; and they believed the scripture and the word which Jesus had spoken.[69]

---

[69] Jn 2:13–22.

I do not intend to do a detailed commentary on this passage, in which, among other things, Jesus announces the substitution of the Jerusalem Temple with his own body as the true sanctuary.[70] We are looking at this text from the particular angle of adoration. It is true that this passage does not use the noun *proskunēsis* or the verb *proskuneō*. However, let us ask ourselves a question: Why does Jesus perform such a dramatic act as to take up a whip and cast the merchants out of the Temple? We must remember the central place of the Jerusalem Temple in the life of the people of Israel. It was the only legitimate sanctuary in which the Jews could offer sacrifices to God.[71] It was Israel's house of prayer *par excellence*, the eminent abode of God's presence. But this shrine was no longer respected as it was meant to be. The problem was not so much that there were animal dealers and money-changers, for they were needed so the Jews could buy animals to offer in sacrifice. The problem was rather how they were situated: they were in the Temple itself, transforming the house of God into a house of trade. The Jerusalem Temple, Israel's most holy place, was no longer respected. This lack of respect clearly denoted a lack of adoration on the part of the Jews. It is the adoration of God that gives someone a sense of the sacred, a sense of the importance of respecting sacred places and times.

This episode was not the first time in Jesus' life that he came to the Temple. After his presentation, he came every year from the age of twelve. So there had been long years during which he witnessed the Jews' lack of respect for his Father's house, and being the Beloved Son, his heart

---

[70] The expulsion of the sheep and oxen may also signify the fact that in the presence of Jesus, the Lamb of God, the Old Testament animal sacrifices become obsolete (see Xavier Léon-Dufour, *Lecture de l'évangile selon Jean*, I, p. 255).

[71] See Dt 12:5–7; 13–14.

grieved over it. Perhaps he had prayed that these people would understand how misplaced their trade was in this holy place, but they had not understood. For this reason, consumed with zeal, Jesus ends up taking the whip to them to drive them from the Temple. With such strong action, he reminded the Jews of the sacredness of the Jerusalem Temple and therefore implicitly of adoration.

We can find confirmation of this interpretation by observing that this episode immediately follows the wedding feast of Cana, where Mary draws her son's attention to the fact that "They have no wine" (Jn 2:3). In the literal sense, this naturally has to do with the physical wine that has run out at the wedding supper. In the spiritual sense, if we consider the symbolism of wine in the nuptial context of the Old Testament, especially in the Song of Songs,[72] we can interpret the wine as a symbol of love. "They have no wine" then means Israel, Yahweh's bride, has run out of love.

The fact that John reports the episode of the cleansing of the Temple nearly at the beginning of Jesus' apostolic life shows us the importance Jesus gave to this act: it was urgent to remind the Jews of the demands of the first commandment of the Law. For Christ, this seems to have been a "pastoral priority."

CONVERSATION WITH THE SAMARITAN WOMAN (JN 4)

Now we turn to Jesus' conversation with the Samaritan woman (Jn 4), which is certainly one of the masterpieces of the Fourth Gospel. Once again I will look at this text from the particular viewpoint of adoration, without giving any overall commentary.[73]

---

[72] See Song 1:2, 4; 4:10.

[73] Ignace de la Potterie is right to underscore the Christological character of the account (see "Jésus et les Samaritains," pp. 34–35), but I will consider it from a particular angle.

Beginning of the Dialogue. We should first notice the situation of the characters at the moment the dialogue begins: Jesus was passing through Samaria; his disciples had gone into the local Samaritan village to buy something to eat, while Jesus, weary from the journey, had sat down at the well. It was around the sixth hour, or noon: "There came a woman of Samaria to draw water. Jesus said to her, 'Give me a drink.'" Let us try to understand the situation. This woman comes to the well alone to draw water at the hottest time of day. This is not really the best time to do such hard work; people usually came to draw water at dawn or sunset. So why did the Samaritan come to the well at noon? We can wonder whether she had purposely chosen that time. If she had come at sundown, she would surely have run into other women of the village. They might have said some unkind things about her, or perhaps even worse. The Samaritan woman's marital status must have been common knowledge, and people must have spoken scornfully of her. So the Samaritan woman preferred coming to the well at a time she knew she would be alone, to avoid people's sarcastic remarks.

But that day, somebody is there, a Jewish man, no less. We observe Jesus' position: he is seated *on* the well.[74] He has positioned himself in such a way that, if the Samaritan woman wishes to draw water, she cannot avoid him. Perhaps the Samaritan woman hesitated a moment. Wouldn't it be better to come back later, in the hope this man might be gone? Yes, but how much time would he stay at the well? He seems weary from his journey. What is more, if the Samaritan woman comes back later, she risks running into the women of the village, which, from her point of view, would be worse. She might have thought to herself, "Oh, well, I'll go to the well now anyway. I'll not say a

---

[74] The use of the Greek preposition *epi* with the dative can be so interpreted.

word to this Jewish man. I'll not even look at him. I'll draw water as quickly as I can, and then I'll be on my way. I prefer that to meeting up with the women of the village." In any case, one thing is certain: the Samaritan woman had no intention of speaking to Jesus, and she expected nothing from him. The proof of this is her astonished reaction when Jesus asks her for something. "'How is it that you, a Jew, ask a drink of me, a woman of Samaria?' For Jews have no dealings with Samaritans."[75]

Preachers know by experience that it is very difficult to preach to an audience with absolutely no interest in what they wish to say and a "Whatever!" frame of mind. So how will Jesus go about touching this woman's heart if she is uninterested in him and expects nothing from him? We can only admire the pastoral intelligence of his approach toward her. He knows he must make the first move, since the woman will not speak first. Jesus begins by asking her for something, something he does not have but that she can give him. He is thirsty and has nothing to draw water, but she has a pitcher; in this way she is superior to Jesus!

The dialogue unfolds in several stages. Jesus takes up the first pastoral challenge, which consists in awakening interest in the woman's heart. He does so by bringing up a mysterious water whose secret he guards. "If you knew the gift of God, and who it is that is saying to you, 'Give me a drink,' you would have asked him and he would have given you living water."[76]

The tactic works, for the woman's curiosity is piqued:

Sir, you have nothing to draw with, and the well is deep; where do you get that living water? Are you greater that our father Jacob, who gave us the well, and drank from it himself, and his sons, and his cattle?[77]

[75] Jn 4:9.   [76] Jn 4:10.   [77] Jn 4:11–12.

Obviously, the Samaritan woman does not understand that Jesus is speaking of spiritual water. She imagines he is talking about physical water and wonders where it could come from. There are a number of examples of such misinterpretations in the Gospel of John;[78] Jesus speaks of spiritual realities, and his hearers take it in a material way, and so Jesus speaks again to dispel the misunderstanding. Meanwhile, the Samaritan woman exhibits a superiority complex, smugly taking advantage of the situation to point out to this Jew one of the glories of the Samaritans: this well had been given to them by Jacob himself.

Jesus answered her:

> *Every one who drinks of this water will thirst again, but whoever drinks of the water that I shall give him will never thirst; the water that I shall give him will become in him a spring of water welling up to eternal life.*[79]

Jesus wants to make her understand that the water he speaks of is not of the same nature as that for which she has come. He speaks of a living wellspring for eternal life. The Samaritan woman, who is still interpreting Jesus' words materially, imagines that Jesus has discovered a spring somewhere that never runs dry. She is interested in this spring, for it would be much less tiring to get water from a spring than to have to draw it from a well: "The woman said to him, 'Sir, give me this water, that I may not thirst, nor come here to draw.'"[80]

The Samaritan woman's reaction is, we must admit, rather weak. It is a reaction of laziness. She looks to spare herself a tiresome chore, so she starts taking an interest in this stranger who, though he is not of that country, curi-

---

[78] Here are some of them: Jn 2:19–21; 3:3–5; 6:26–28; 8:21–22.
[79] Jn 4:13–14.
[80] Jn 4:15.

ously knows of a spring of which she knows nothing. This is an example of temporal messianism, that is, the tendency to reduce Jesus' mission from the spiritual level to a purely material level. Another striking example may be found in the Fourth Gospel's multiplication of the loaves. After Jesus feeds the multitude bread and fish, the impulse of the people is to get their hands on him in the hope that he will do the same thing again. It is great to get free bread and fish every day! Nobody has to work anymore! No doubt, the loaves and fishes were delicious, since the Lord did all things well. Jesus is obliged to correct them; he has not come to dispense people from work but to give them the true bread from Heaven:

> *Truly, truly, I say to you, you seek me, not because you saw signs, but because you ate your fill of the loaves. Do not labor for the food which perishes, but for the food which endures to eternal life, which the Son of man will give to you; for on him has God the Father set his seal.*[81]

As far as the Samaritan woman is concerned, Jesus did not come to dispense her from work. His mission is absolutely not that of an engineer called in to solve water supply problems! In a word, the Samaritan woman's reaction is not exactly brilliant. However, she has made considerable progress from the beginning of the encounter, for *now she asks for something* from Jesus. She does indeed make a mistake regarding the nature of the living water, but at least she asks for something, whereas before she had expected nothing from Jesus and asked nothing of him.

Then comes a turning point in the dialogue: "Jesus said to her, 'Go, call your husband and come here.'" But why does Jesus say this to the Samaritan woman? What connection could there be between the living water and her

---

[81] Jn 6:26–27.

husband? Furthermore, Jesus' questions might seem imprudent. If we were able to give Jesus a bit of advice, knowing the Samaritan woman's marital status, we surely would have said, "Careful, Lord! Don't broach that subject. It's much too sensitive. The woman might withdraw into herself just when she had started opening up." In other words, Jesus seems to do something unpastoral. Naturally, it is nothing of the sort; his request springs from his wisdom. But let us acknowledge that the connection between the living water and the husband is not an obvious one, since the evangelist does not explain. We must try to understand. It is odd that the rest of the account makes no allusion to living water. What continuity is there between the beginning of the account, which speaks of water, and the rest of it, having to do with the husband? What follows of the dialogue helps us to guess the profound reason for Jesus' question: the woman answers, "I have no husband." We would need to be able to hear her tone of voice; it is certainly not a neutral tone, but more likely the harsh tone of someone who dislikes Jesus' question. The woman's response must mean something like, "Don't invade my private life. It's none of your business." So the woman starts turning in on herself, but Jesus moves more quickly and catches her up. "Jesus said to her, 'You are right in saying, "I have no husband"; for you have had five husbands, and he whom you now have is not your husband; this you said truly.' "[82]

Jesus puts the Samaritan woman *before the truth of her life*: she is living in sin, having had multiple husbands and now living with a new partner who is not her husband. We begin to understand the link between the living water and the husband. The Samaritan woman hoped to receive a material benefit from Jesus, one that involved no new de-

---

[82] Jn 4:17–18.

mands. On the contrary, Jesus wants to show her that the gift he wishes to give her involves a demand for truth and conversion. The Samaritan woman cannot just receive the living water and keep living the life she's living, which is a life of sin. The Samaritan woman did not expect this. She had never met this Jewish man before and was worlds away from suspecting that he knew her life's deepest secrets. It is clear that Jesus could not reveal this to her immediately, or she would have run off right away. But now she understands that she is in the presence of a prophet, for it was impossible for a stranger she had never met to know the secrets of her private life.

Teaching on Adoration in Spirit and Truth. "The woman said to him, 'Sir, I perceive that you are a prophet. Our fathers worshiped on this mountain; and you say that in Jerusalem is the place where man ought to worship.'"[83] We come to a second turning point in the dialogue. Once more, the connection between what has gone before and what follows is not obvious. Jesus and the Samaritan woman now start talking about adoration, seemingly forgetting all about the husband. Again, however, the link is real, but it must be brought out. Why does the Samaritan woman ask Jesus this question about adoration? Because she is confronted with a prophet and wants to tell him what is troubling her heart. The Samaritans were in the habit of offering their sacrifices "on this mountain," that is, on Mount Gerizim in Samaria, where they had built a rival sanctuary to the one in Jerusalem. The Jews, on the other hand, faithful to the teaching of Deuteronomy insisted on the fact that the only legitimate shrine was the Jerusalem Temple, hence the liturgical quarrel that existed between them. The Samaritan woman was a witness to all of this. In

[83] Jn 4:19–20.

her youth she must have felt in her heart the desire to adore God. The only problem was, she had heard violently contradictory opinions. Some said, "Do you want to worship God? Then you must go to Jerusalem." Others said, "No! There's no point going to Jerusalem; go up to Gerizim." The poor woman was lost, not knowing what to do, perhaps afraid to displease God. She must have stopped adoring. We could think that the five husbands are only a consequence of the fact that she stopped adoring God. In other words, since her heart could no longer satisfy its natural aspiration to adore God, it sought emotional compensations. The Samaritan woman started multiplying partners, unable to quench her heart's thirst for love.

How will Jesus save this poor woman whose heart has been so deeply wounded? It is striking that he does not preach to her about morality or the law. Jesus does not tell her, "That's so wrong. You're living in sin. Adultery is punished by the Law of Moses. You have to get rid of your current partner." Of course, adultery is evil, and it is condemned by the Law, but Jesus intervenes at a deeper level. He does not treat the Samaritan woman's problem by focusing on the effects but by focusing on the *cause*. The woman has to start adoring again, and she has to adore in a new way, in spirit and truth:

> *Jesus said to her, "Woman, believe me, the hour is coming when neither on this mountain nor in Jerusalem will you worship the Father. You worship what you do not know; we worship what we know, for salvation is from the Jews. But the hour is coming, and now is, when the true worshipers will worship the Father in spirit and truth, for such the Father seeks to worship him. God is spirit, and those who worship him must worship in spirit and truth." The woman said to him, "I know that Messiah is coming (he who is called Christ); when he comes, he will show us all things." Jesus said to her, "I who speak to you am he."*[84]

[84] Jn 4:21–26.

Jesus explicitly reveals himself to the Samaritan woman as the Messiah. The teaching he gives her is therefore a *messianic teaching*; it is part of Christ's messianic mission. Jesus has come to earth to teach adoration in spirit and truth. This tells us the importance of this Gospel passage, which is unique. Let us try to understand this adoration in spirit and truth. The crucial expression "in spirit and truth" may be interpreted in various ways.

First of all, a primary sense of "adoration in spirit and truth" can have to do with the spiritual character of the act of adoration and its demand for truth before God. Adoration is not first a question of place, as if the Samaritan woman could only adore in one specific place designated by God, whether it be the Jerusalem Temple or Mount Gerizim. Adoration must be "in spirit," in the sense that it must be a loving act of will that a human being can do anywhere.[85] Adoration is not limited to the offering of an animal sacrifice, which presupposes an approved shrine; it has a much broader extension. Wherever he is, man can adore God in his heart, and this is what is most important; the offering of a material sacrifice is secondary. Moreover, adoration has a demand for truth: the person who adores God must have an upright intention toward him, in particular the intention to conform his life to the demands of the covenant, as formulated by the Law of Moses. The prophets of Israel reminded the Jews that it is not enough to offer God a material sacrifice; one's heart has to be in it, lest God abhor the sacrifice. God refuses the sacrifices of those who perform the purely outward action of sacrifice without taking care to conform their lives to the covenant. We find an eloquent testimony to this fact at the beginning of the Book of Isaiah:

---

[85] This is the interpretation found in St. Augustine (*Homilies on the Gospel of John*, XV, 24).

What to me is the multitude of your sacrifices? says the Lord; I have had enough of burnt offerings of rams and the fat of fed beasts; I do not delight in the blood of bulls, or of lambs, or of he-goats.

When you come to appear before me, who requires of you this trampling of my courts? Bring no more vain offerings; incense is an abomination to me. . . . When you spread forth your hands, I will hide my eyes from you; even though you make many prayers, I will not listen. . . . Remove the evil of your doings from before my eyes; cease to do evil, learn to do good. [86]

Another text of the same kind is found in Psalm 50(49):

The Mighty One, God the Lord, speaks and summons the earth. . . . "Gather to me my faithful ones, who made a covenant with me by sacrifice! . . . Hear, O my people, and I will speak, O Israel, I will testify against you. I am God, your God. I do not reprove you for your sacrifices; your burnt offerings are continually before me. I will accept no bull from your house, nor he-goat from your folds. For every beast of the forest is mine, the cattle on a thousand hills. . . . If I were hungry, I would not tell you; for the world and all that is in it is mine. Do I eat the flesh of bulls, or drink the blood of goats? Offer to God a sacrifice of thanksgiving, and pay your vows to the Most High." [87]

In the New Covenant, adoration is to be even more "in spirit and truth"; it must be a spiritual act of man truly expressing his real love for the Lord and not a purely material act in which man does not put his whole heart.

In a second sense, we may understand adoration in spirit and truth as a demand of purity in faith. We ought to notice how in this dialogue Jesus makes no compromise about the truth. In today's theological language, we would say that the Samaritan woman is a "separated sister." Jesus has mercy on her, but he also has her understand that the Samaritans adore one whom they do not know, while the

---

[86] Is 1:11–16.   [87] Ps 50(49):1–14.

Jews, for their part, adore one they do know.[88] The Samaritans' faith did not have the same purity as that of the Jews. On the one hand, they only recognized the Pentateuch as Sacred Scripture; on the other, their faith was slightly contaminated by pagan doctrines, by reason of their historical origin: the Samaritans were the descendants of the tribes that the King of Assyria had sent from the region of Babylon to replace the Israelites deported after the sack of Samaria in 721 B.C. These peoples honored Yahweh along with other pagan divinities.[89] The Jews, on the contrary, had preserved the purity of faith in Yahweh, the God of Israel. The Father wills to be adored in truth, that is, with a pure faith, not a faith contaminated with errors; errors in religious doctrine, far from being neutral, are obstacles to faith and so also inevitably obstacles to love.[90]

We can also interpret adoration "in spirit" in another way, by understanding it as adoration "in the Spirit," that is, in the Holy Spirit. We must not forget that in the most ancient Greek manuscripts of the New Testament the text is entirely written in capital letters; the translators were the ones who chose between "in spirit" and "in the Spirit." Might Jesus be speaking of the Holy Spirit here? Indeed, the living water of which he spoke in the first part of the conversation does seem to make allusion to the Holy Spirit. We cannot fail to miss the link between this text and the following passage of the Fourth Gospel:

> On the last day of the feast, the great day, Jesus stood up and proclaimed, "If any one thirst, let him come to me and drink. He who believes in me, as the scripture has said, 'Out of his heart shall

---

[88] We find this interpretation in St. Thomas Aquinas (*Commentary on the Gospel of John*, I, 603–610).

[89] See 2 Kgs 17:24–41.

[90] I have developed this point in my book *Les Vertus théologales*, pp. 40–47.

flow rivers of living water.'" Now this he said about the Spirit,
which those who believed in him were to receive; for as yet the
Spirit had not been given, because Jesus was not yet glorified. [91]

This passage from chapter 7 is the only other text in the
Gospel of John that mentions living water. Furthermore,
the water Jesus will give will be a spring welling up to
eternal life (Jn 4:14); it is the Spirit who gives life (Jn
6:63).[92]

However, it should be noted that the Holy Spirit is to
be given *after* the glorification of Jesus. It is therefore
probable that the meaning of the expression "gift of God"
is twofold and alludes to the present gift offered to the
Samaritan woman of the revelation of Jesus ("If you knew
the gift of God, and who it is that is saying to you"; "I who
speak to you am he"), a revelation into which the gift of the
Spirit after Easter will enable us to enter more deeply. In
fact, the Old Testament sometimes designates the discourse of wisdom as a fountain of living water.[93] Jesus' first
gift to the woman is therefore that of the revelation of his
person. This gift will be deepened by the gift of the Spirit
(in 4:13-14, the verbs are in the future tense). It is therefore also right to see an allusion to the Holy Spirit in the
expression "adore in spirit and truth"; this means that the
Holy Spirit is to play a role in adoration in the New Covenant.[94] We shall return to this point in the theological
part of this book.

Finally, to come back to "adoration in truth," we can

---

[91] Jn 7:37–39.

[92] We might also add the following argument: the expression "gift of God"
designates the Holy Spirit in Acts 8:20, in which the scene is situated in
Samaria.

[93] Prov 13:14; 16:22; 18:4; Sir 24:30ff.

[94] We find this interpretation in Origen (*Commentary on St. John*, XIII, 109)
and in John Scotus Erigena (ninth century) in his *Commentary on the Gospel of
John*, IV, 7 (*Sources Chrétiennes* 180, p. 319).

look for an interpretation that takes the proper characteristics of Johannine theology into greater account. In particular, we ought to consider the fact that, in John's Gospel, Jesus designates himself as the truth: "I am the way, and the truth, and the life" (Jn 14:6). For St. John, Jesus is the Truth in the sense that he is the perfect revelation of the Father: "No one has ever seen God; the only Son, who is in the bosom of the Father, he has made him known" (Jn 1:18). On the other hand, it is striking to see that God is rarely invoked as Father in the Old Testament, especially in an individual person's invocation.[95] One of the rare exceptions is found in Psalm 89(88), in which the Psalmist says of the descendent of David, who will be the Messiah: "He shall cry to me, 'You are my Father, my God and the Rock of my salvation.' And I will make him the first-born, the highest of the kings of the earth" (Ps 89[88]:27-28). Therefore, it was something new to hear Jesus pray to God and call him "Abba, Father."[96] Now in his conversation with the Samaritan woman, Jesus does not speak of adoring God, but of *adoring the Father*. In the light of this fact, should we not understand adoration "in truth" as adoration in union with Jesus, *the* Adorer of the Father? We find confirmation of this in John 4:22: "You worship what you do not know; we worship what we know, for salvation is from the Jews." Who is the "we" of which Jesus speaks? Many commentators think it is the Jews, as opposed to the Samaritans ("you"). Indeed, the Jews did know God better than the Samaritans, to the extent that their faith was purer, as we saw earlier. This interpretation is plausible, yet it presents a difficulty, for Jesus says several times in the Gospel of John that the Jews do not know God:

---

[95] Beyond Ps 89(88):27, we find just three texts, noteworthy for their late redaction: Sir 23:4; Wis 14:3. For a collective invocation of God as Father, see, for example, Is 63:16.

[96] See Mk 14:36.

The Father who sent me has himself borne witness to me. His voice you have never heard, his form you have never seen; and you do not have his word abiding in you. . . .
    You know neither me nor my Father; if you knew me, you would know my Father also. . . .
    It is my Father who glorifies me, of whom you say that he is your God. But you have not known him; I know him. If I said, I do not know him, I should be a liar like you; but I do know him and I keep his word.[97]

In this case, should we not interpret the "we" of John 4: 22 as referring to Jesus himself? He is in fact the perfect adorer in spirit and truth! We might be tempted to think that, to be more explicit, Jesus should have expressed himself in the singular: "I adore what I know."[98] However, another explanation is possible: Jesus might be identifying himself with the "we," and the use of the first person plural might be intentional and meant to solemnize his testimony and attest to his authority, as in Jn 3:11: "Truly, truly, I say to you, we speak of what we know, and bear witness to what we have seen; but you do not receive our testimony."[99]

Whether the "we" of Jn 4: 22 is understood one way or the other, one thing is clear: Jesus is indeed the first adorer in spirit and truth. But, on the other hand, verses 23 and 24 speak in the future tense of other adorers:

But the hour is coming, and now is, when the true worshipers will worship the Father in spirit and truth, for such the Father seeks to

[97] Jn 5:37–38; 8:19, 54–55.
[98] See Ignace de la Potterie, " 'Nous adorons, nous, ce que nous connaissons, car le salut vient des juifs'. Histoire de l'exégèse et interprétation de Jn 4, 22", p. 97. According to this author, this was already the position of St. Cyril of Alexandria.
[99] On the use of "we" instead of "I" as a witness to authority, see: Richard Bauckham, *Jesus and the Eyewitnesses*, ch. 14 ("The Gospel of John as Eyewitness Testimony"), pp. 369–383.

worship him. God is spirit, and those who worship him must worship in spirit and truth.

Here it is clear that this is not about Jesus, but about the adorers he will raise up by his messianic teaching—no doubt, including the Samaritan woman. These adorers will not only adore as Jesus does, but will do so in him ("in truth"). In this regard, it is significant that, in the episode of the cleansing of the Temple that we saw earlier, Jesus suggests that he is the new Temple that will replace the Jerusalem Temple. He is therefore the new place—a spiritual place—in which perfect worship is given to God. (We shall return to this point in the theological part of this book.)

It would be impossible to exaggerate the importance of this messianic teaching of Jesus, which is one of the jewels of the Gospel of St. John. Jesus, as the Messiah, comes to teach adoration in spirit and truth, an adoration which he himself lives fully and of which he is the model. He invites his disciples to enter into his adoration of the Father. This adoration has a saving dimension: Christ comes to raise the Samaritan woman up by setting free the thirst within her to adore God. From this moment, she will become progressively able to bring order into the disordered life of her affections.

HEAVENLY ADORATION IN REVELATION 4

Let us now go on to the Book of Revelation, of which we can truly say that it is the book on adoration *par excellence,* since this theme is present so frequently.[100] We shall not

---

[100] I have made a detailed exegetical study of the passages of Revelation having to do with adoration in the article *"L'Adoration dans l'Apocalypse"* in the book *Chemins à travers l'Apocalypse*; I take the liberty of referring the reader to this work for more details.

look at all the parts of Revelation that deal with adoration, but only some of the most important, in particular chapters 4 and 13.

Chapter 4 of Revelation gives us, in symbolic language, a wonderful description of Heaven. Caught up in ecstasy by the action of the Holy Spirit, John first sees God the Father's throne: "Lo, a throne stood in Heaven, with one seated on the throne! And he who sat there appeared like jasper and carnelian, and round the throne was a rainbow that looked like an emerald."[101] God is not named but is designated as "one seated on the throne." This reserve may be explained by the great respect traditionally shown by Jews for the name of God, but also because it is simply impossible to describe God. John can only suggest the divine splendor by making comparisons drawn from the reflection of light in precious stones.

"Round the throne were twenty-four thrones, and seated on the thrones were twenty-four elders, clad in white garments, with golden crowns upon their heads."[102] These elders are most probably human beings. Their number, twenty-four, is symbolic and expresses the unity between the Old Covenant (the twelve tribes of Jacob being at the origin of Israel) and the New Covenant (the twelve Apostles at the origin of the Church).

From the throne issue flashes of lightning, and voices and peals of thunder, and before the throne burn seven torches of fire, which are the seven spirits of God; and before the throne there is as it were a sea of glass, like crystal.[103]

The lightning, voices, and thunder refer back to the theophany of Sinai in Exodus. The seven spirits of God, symbolized by seven torches of fire, are most probably a symbolic representation of the Holy Spirit in his full-

---

[101] Rev 4:2–3.   [102] Rev 4:4.   [103] Rev 4:5–6a.

ness, expressed by the number seven. Unlike "the Spirit," "the seven spirits" in Revelation designate the Holy Spirit inasmuch as he is sent by Christ.[104] As for the crystal sea, this is a symbol that can be interpreted at different levels. First, we can see in it an allusion to the translucent vault under God's throne in the theophanies of Sinai (Ex 24) and on the banks of the river Chebar in the Book of Ezekiel (Ez 1). If we were to do a Christian application of the symbolism, we might see in it an image of the waters of baptism, according to the common interpretation of the Latin patristic and medieval commentators on Revelation. Finally, an image of Mary may also be seen in it.[105]

> *Round the throne, on each side of the throne, are four living creatures, full of eyes in front and behind: the first living creature like a lion, the second living creature like an ox, the third living creature with the face of a man, and the fourth living creature like a flying eagle. And the four living creatures, each of them with six wings, are full of eyes all round and within, and day and night they never cease to sing, "Holy, holy, holy, is the Lord God Almighty, who was and is and is to come!"*[106]

Nearly all exegetes see in the four living beings the angels who are nearest God's throne. It is true that their description resembles, in a simplified way, the traits found in the seraphim of Isaiah (Is 6: 1-3) and the cherubim of Ezekiel (Ez 1). We shall return to this point in a moment. These living beings praise God by proclaiming his holiness unceasingly. Their praise brings about the adoration of the twenty-four elders:

> *And whenever the living creatures give glory and honor and thanks to him who is seated on the throne, who lives for ever and*

---

[104] See Richard Bauckham, *The Theology of the Book of Revelation*, ch. 5 ("The Spirit of Prophecy").

[105] See my detailed study in the article "*La Mer de cristal dans l'Apocalypse*," published in *Chemins à travers l'Apocalypse*.

[106] Rev 4:6b–8.

*ever, the twenty-four elders fall down before him who is seated on
the throne and worship him who lives for ever and ever; they cast
their crowns before the throne, singing, "Worthy are you, our Lord
and God, to receive glory and honor and power, for you created all
things, and by your will they existed and were created."* [107]

The glory and thanksgiving that the living beings offer
to God inspire the elders to make the significant act of
prostration in view of adoring God. The elders' song es-
tablishes an explicit connection between their adoration
and the fact that the one whom they adore is he who created all things. It is indeed *as Creator* that they adore God.
Let us also note another symbolic action: that of casting
one's crown before God's throne. This homage is a way of
acknowledging that the nobility and glory of the elders
were given to them by God as a free gift, and of offering
them back to God.

We therefore have in this passage a most beautiful description of heavenly adoration. This adoration is given
"day and night," for it accompanies the living beings'
praise. In Heaven God is adored unceasingly; all are in a
permanent act of adoration. If such is life in Heaven, is it
not fitting to begin adoring God on earth? [108]

We said earlier that the living beings were usually interpreted as being angels near God's throne (or even, according to some commentators, holding up this throne).
This is a common interpretation, but it is not entirely
satisfying. We may wonder, in fact, whether the four living beings are not actually a Christological symbol, that
is, a symbolic representation of Christ. I have given a detailed exegetical argument in favor of the Christological

---

[107] Rev 4:9–11.

[108] This is what St. Teresa of the Andes came to understand: "In Heaven, the
occupation of souls will be to adore and to love. Let us begin, then, on earth
what we'll be doing for all eternity!" (Letter 101 of May 14, 1919, to Elisa
Valdés Ossa, *Letters of Saint Teresa of the Andes*, p. 228).

interpretation elsewhere,[109] and here briefly sum up a few essential points.

First of all, the fact that there are four living beings poses no difficulty. In symbolic language, a specific symbol does not signify a specific person but a specific function. Consequently, the presence of four different symbols in the text does not imply the existence of four different persons; it could very well be the same person seen from four different points of view.[110] For the same reason, the fact that Christ is represented by the symbol of the Lamb in chapter 5 does not prevent his being represented in another way in chapter 4.

Next, let us observe that the four symbols used for the living beings each express a high-point of creation: the lion is the king of beasts, the bull is the strongest animal,[111] man is the most intelligent animal, and the eagle is the animal that flies highest. Now, isn't Christ the high-point of the created universe?

Third, these living beings occupy a strange position, for they are at once "in the midst of the throne and around the throne" of God. This expression is a real puzzle for some commentators, for it seems contradictory: how can one be at once in the middle of the throne and yet around it? It seems impossible. Moreover, what would angels be doing in the middle of God's throne? According to the Book of Revelation, the only beings to occupy God's throne are God himself and the Lamb, which everyone understands to be Christ. It is hard to grasp why angels would take this place. In fact, this situation becomes clearer within a Christological interpretation: as equal to God in dignity, Christ can occupy God's throne; as man, he stands at the

---

[109] See "*L'Adoration dans l'Apocalypse*," I, pp. 95–105.

[110] On this point, see my study "*Le Langage symbolique de l'Apocalypse*," published in *Chemins à travers l'Apocalypse*.

[111] In the limited experience of the Jews at the time of Revelation, naturally.

same time with creatures, which are around the throne. This is a lovely way to express non-conceptually through the use of symbolic images what will later become the theological doctrine of the divine and human natures of Christ.

And finally, what is the function of the four living beings? They seem to preside over heavenly adoration, for at the signal of their praise the elders adore God. Let us ask the question theologically: Who presides in Heaven over the heavenly worship? Angels? Is it not rather Christ as man?[112]

I would like to point out that the Christological interpretation of the living beings in the Book of Revelation is not something new. It is, in fact, ancient, for we find it among the Church Fathers, in Victorinus of Pettau (third century) and St. Ambrose of Milan (fourth century).[113] But it has largely been forgotten; much better remembered is the interpretation of St. Irenaeus, who sees in the four living beings the four evangelists. This latter interpretation is doubtless not the primary sense of the text, but it may be considered a derived sense to the extent that the

[112] Theologically, it is unfitting for Christ *as God* to adore the Father, but it does befit him *as man*, not because he is a creature, but because he takes on a created human nature. Earlier, we saw that Jesus' statement in Jn 4:22 ("You worship what you do not know; we worship what we know, for salvation is from the Jews.") designated Christ as the first adorer of the Father.

[113] "Indeed, he [Christ] had been proclaimed as a lion and as a lion's whelp [Gn 49:9]. For the salvation of humankind he was made man for the defeat of death and for the liberation of all. Because he offered himself as a sacrifice to God the Father for us, he is called a calf. And because, when death was conquered, he ascended into the Heavens and held out his wings to cover his people, he is called an eagle in flight" (Victorinus of Pettau, *Commentary on the Apocalypse*, IV, 4, p. 7). "However, many think that our Lord himself is represented by the figure of the four animals. He is attested to be a man, he a lion, he a bull calf; he an eagle. He is a man, because he was born of Mary; a lion, because he is strong; a bull calf, because he is the victim; an eagle, because he is the resurrection." (Ambrose of Milan, *Expositionis in Evangelium secundum Lucam libri X*, I, prologue, 8, col. 1612.)

four evangelists give the whole Church four portraits of Christ. In exegesis it is difficult to offer an irrefutable demonstration of a given interpretation. This is even truer in the case of a book that systematically uses symbolic language. The Christological interpretation seems to have the upper hand over the angelic interpretation because of the convergence of clues, although it is not without difficulties. If it is exact, the consequence that must be drawn about heavenly adoration is easily understood: Christ is indeed the one who directs the continual adoration of the Father. This conclusion displays remarkably full coherence with the interpretation of John 4 above.

ADORATION AND PRAISE (REV 5)

Chapter 4 of Revelation shows us heavenly adoration directed by the four living beings. God the Father ("the one seated on the throne") is adored as the Creator. Chapter 5 of Revelation presents to us a new adoration at the moment the Lamb takes the sealed scroll from the Father's hand:

> *He [the Lamb] went and took the scroll from the right hand of him who was seated on the throne. And when he had taken the scroll, the four living creatures and the twenty-four elders fell down before the Lamb, each holding a harp, and with golden bowls full of incense, which are the prayers of the saints; and they sang a new song, saying,*
> *"Worthy are you to take the scroll and open its seals, for you were slain and by thy blood ransomed men for God from every tribe and tongue and people and nation, and have made them a kingdom and priests to our God, and they shall reign on earth."*
> *Then I looked, and I heard around the throne and the living creatures and the elders the voice of many angels, numbering myriads of myriads and thousands of thousands, saying with a loud voice, "Worthy is the Lamb who was slain, to receive power and*

*wealth and wisdom and might and honor and glory and blessing!
And I heard every creature in Heaven and on earth and under the
earth and in the sea, and all therein, saying, "To him who sits upon
the throne and to the Lamb be blessing and honor and glory and
might for ever and ever!" And the four living creatures said,
"Amen!" and the elders fell down and worshiped.*[114]

Let us note several new elements compared to the adoration of chapter 4. First of all, the main thing that is new
is that Christ (under the figure of the Lamb, the major
Christological symbol of the Book of Revelation) is adored
equally with God. The canticle of the elders also mentions
the redemptive work he accomplished for the salvation of
mankind. On the other hand, angels take part in the heavenly adoration. Finally, the text mentions praises and liturgical objects (bowls, incense, harps, and so on). What is
shown is no longer simply heavenly adoration but heavenly liturgy; this follows adoration and is rooted in it. Here
we have a precious indication about the way earthly liturgy
is to unfold.

ADORATION OF THE BEAST (REV 13)

Revelation 4 showed us the great importance of adoration
in Heaven. We can be persuaded of the importance of
adoration in a wholly different way, by way of contrast,
by looking at how the Devil does everything he can to
turn human beings away from adoring God. Revelation 13
gives us an impressive glimpse of this, as we shall now
see.

Chapter 12 presented the figure of the Dragon for the
first time. It is explicitly stated that this is "that ancient

---

[114] Rev 5:7–14. On the meaning of the "fall" of the four living beings before
the Lamb, which must not be interpreted as adoration but as self-effacement,
see the discussion in *"L'Adoration dans l'Apocalypse," Chemins à travers l'Apocalypse*, pp. 100–101.

serpent, who is called the Devil or Satan, the deceiver of the whole world" (Rev 12:9). At the beginning of chapter 13, once the Dragon has been cast down from Heaven to earth, John sees two Beasts rise up, one after the other:

And I saw a beast rising out of the sea, with ten horns and seven heads, with ten diadems upon its horns and a blasphemous name upon its heads. And the beast that I saw was like a leopard, its feet were like a bear's, and its mouth was like a lion's mouth. And to it the dragon gave his power and his throne and great authority. One of its heads seemed to have a mortal wound, but its mortal wound was healed, and the whole earth followed the beast with wonder. Men worshiped the dragon, for he had given his authority to the beast, and they worshiped the beast, saying, "Who is like the beast, and who can fight against it?"

And the beast was given a mouth uttering haughty and blasphemous words, and it was allowed to exercise authority for forty-two months; it opened its mouth to utter blasphemies against God, blaspheming his name and his dwelling, that is, those who dwell in Heaven. Also it was allowed to make war on the saints and to conquer them. And authority was given it over every tribe and people and tongue and nation, and all who dwell on earth will worship it, every one whose name has not been written before the foundation of the world in the book of life of the Lamb that was slain....

Then I saw another beast which rose out of the earth; it had two horns like a lamb and it spoke like a dragon. It exercises all the authority of the first beast in its presence, and makes the earth and its inhabitants worship the first beast, whose mortal wound was healed. It works great signs, even making fire come down from Heaven to earth in the sight of men; and by the sign which it is allowed to work in the presence of the beast, it deceives those who dwell on earth, bidding them make an image for the beast which was wounded by the sword and yet lived; and it was allowed to give breath to the image of the beast so that the image of the beast should even speak, and to cause those who would not worship the image of the beast to be slain.[115]

---

[115] Rev 13:1–8, 11–15.

It is not hard to guess that what we have here is an anti-Trinity, in which the Dragon, Satan, is a demonic caricature of the Father; the first Beast, or the Beast from the sea, is a caricature of Christ; and the second Beast, the Beast from the land, is a caricature of the Holy Spirit. Just as the Father has handed over all authority to the Son, the Dragon has handed over all authority to the Beast from the Sea. Just as the Holy Spirit leads people to Christ, the Beast from the land seeks to lead them to the Beast from the sea. Finally, just as Christ the Lamb bears the marks of his Passion (Rev 5:6), so the Beast from the sea bears a mortal wound but has come back to life.

It may be said that these two Beasts are two "creatures" of the Devil that he raises up to achieve his purposes more effectively. But what is his objective? It is stated clearly enough: "Men worshiped the dragon, for he had given his authority to the beast, and they worshiped the beast, saying, 'Who is like the beast, and who can fight against it?'"[116] In other words, *what Satan seeks is for human beings to adore him instead of adoring God.* In the madness of his pride, he claims man's adoration. Let us observe in this respect that the episode of the temptation of Jesus in the desert already showed the same thing:

> *Again, the devil took him to a very high mountain, and showed him all the kingdoms of the world and the glory of them; and he said to him, "All these I will give you, if you will fall down and worship me." Then Jesus said to him, "Be gone, Satan! For it is written, 'You shall worship the Lord your God and him only shall you serve.'"*[117]

To attain his objectives, the Dragon raises up the Beasts to frighten and seduce humanity and turn it away from

---

[116] It is easy to see how the cry "Who is like the Beast?" is the demonic caricature of the name "Michael" (meaning "who is like God?"), who appears in Rev 12:7.

[117] Mt 4:8–10; see also Lk 4:7–8.

God. What are the means he uses? We find three of them:

— *Power.* He raises up an extremely powerful Beast (described with traits from three wild animals: the panther, the bear, and the lion) that seems impossible to resist. In fact, all who choose to resist it are pitilessly slain.

— *Prodigious signs* striking people's imaginations.

— *Idolatrous liturgy*, organized and orchestrated by the Beast from the earth.

This scene is extremely instructive. The Devil knows that the desire to adore is deeply anchored in the human heart. He does not seek to eliminate this desire, but to take control of it and thus use it for his purposes, to his profit alone. It is as though the Devil were telling people, "Do you want to adore? That's fine. But do not adore God! Adore the Beast (and me too)."

All of this is shown in symbolic language. We might wonder what the specific meaning of all this might be. Historically speaking, first of all, we can look for the possible meaning of this scene for the first Christians for whom Revelation was written, those who lived in the seven churches of Asia Minor at the end of the first century A.D. We usually think, doubtless rightly, that Revelation alludes to the cult of the emperor, which flourished particularly in Asia Minor at that time. Julius Caesar had already been declared a god after his death in 44 B.C. His successor, Augustus, granted the Roman provinces of Asia and Bithynia permission to erect temples in Ephesus and Nicaea for the veneration of the Spirit of Rome and the deified Julius Caesar. After him, it became common to deify the Roman emperors after their deaths,[118] and a number of

---

[118] It is reported that Emperor Vespasian (who died in 79 A.D.) said with black humor on his deathbed, "*Vae, puto deus fio*" ("Woe, I think I am becoming

cities, including Smyrna, requested authorization to build temples in the emperors' honor. Domitian marked a turning point; he reigned from 81 to 96 A.D. and was surely the emperor reigning at the time of the Book of Revelation. Unlike his predecessors, Domitian demanded to be called a god during his lifetime.[119] It is easy to understand that such a claim was unacceptable to the Christians, who recognized only one God. It therefore seems Revelation was a polemic against the Roman Empire to the extent that it propagated, encouraged, and even demanded the idolatrous cult of the emperor. In this respect, exegetes usually see in the Beast from the sea the Roman Empire itself [120] and, in the Beast from the land, the imperial cult.

This historical interpretation is interesting, but it does not exhaust the meaning of the text. The Roman Empire and the cult of the emperor are the first manifestations of the Beasts, their first historical "incarnations," so to speak. However, by contemporizing the text, we can find other manifestations of the Beasts throughout history. How could we not think in particular of the totalitarian political regimes of the twentieth century, which not only persecuted Christians but went so far as to promote a veritable "personality cult" of the head of state, even organizing idolatrous pseudo-liturgies?[121] In our day, we cannot fail to mention the actual worship of Satan that is openly asserting itself.

Revelation 13 is striking. It contains an important teaching on adoration, but it communicates it by way of

---

a god"). He meant he was near to being declared a god inasmuch as he was near death.

[119] According to the historian Suetonius, Domitian had himself called "*Dominus ac Deus noster*" ("Our Lord and God").

[120] In fact, this Beast takes on the traits of the first three ferocious beasts of Dn 7:1–6, which symbolized pagan empires.

[121] I am thinking of Hitler, Stalin, Ceaucescu, Mao-Tse-Tung, and so on.

contrast: we see the antithesis of the adoration of God, which Revelation showed us in its vision of Heaven in chapter 4. In Heaven, men and angels live full and perfect adoration under the leadership of the four living beings. The adoration of the Beast is the demonic caricature of the adoration of God. The Devil, under the figure of the Dragon, does everything he can to turn people away from their adoration of God and to give their adoration to himself alone. As the Devil is remarkably intelligent, his strategy makes us understand better just how important the adoration of God is.

ADORATION RESERVED TO GOD (REV 19 AND 22)

Near the end of Revelation, we find two curious and similar passages in which John tries to adore the angel who is speaking to him:

> *And the angel said to me, "Write this: Blessed are those who are invited to the marriage supper of the Lamb." And he said to me, "These are true words of God." Then I fell down at his feet to worship him, but he said to me, "You must not do that! I am a fellow servant with you and your brethren who hold the testimony of Jesus. Worship God." For the testimony of Jesus is the spirit of prophecy.*[122]

> *I John am he who heard and saw these things. And when I heard and saw them, I fell down to worship at the feet of the angel who showed them to me; but he said to me, "You must not do that! I am a fellow servant with you and your brethren the prophets, and with those who keep the words of this book. Worship God.*[123]

John's action is quite amazing. How can he make such a "mistake," and two times at that, even though he had been corrected the first time? Is it a case of mistaken identity of

---

[122] Rev 19:9–10.   [123] Rev 22:8–9.

the one speaking to him? Nothing in the text suggests the angel is divine, like Christ.[124] It is more fitting to think that it is a symbolic double scene meant to transmit this theological teaching insistently: adoration must be reserved for God and cannot be given to angels.[125]

The Old Testament repeatedly shows us scenes in which an angel appears to a human being; nearly always, the one who sees the angel bows down before him: Abraham before the three men (Gen 18:2), Lot in Sodom (Gen 19:1), Balaam (Num 22:31), Joshua (Jos 5:14), Manoah and his wife (Jdg 13:20), David (1Chr 20:16), Tobias and Tobit before Raphael (Tob 12:16), Daniel before the man clothed in linen (Dan 10: 9). Furthermore, the angel never refuses this gesture saying that the human being should reserve it for God. In the New Testament, on the other hand, we do not see any human being give the proskynesis to an angel. For example, in the Gospel of Luke, Zechariah and Mary do not bow down before the angel Gabriel. Likewise, the women who come to Jesus' tomb on the morning of the Resurrection, do not bow down before the Angel of the Lord,[126] but they do so before Jesus (cf. Mt 28:9). Unlike the Old Testament, the New Testament *de facto* reserves proskynesis to God (including Christ). If now in Revelation, for the first time in the New Testament, a man wants to give the proskynesis to an angel and the angel refuses it, it seems that the teaching is indeed that the gesture of proskynesis is no longer suitable. There are actions that may be acceptable in the Old Testament context but are no longer so in the New Testament context. Here are two lovely passages from

---

[124] Let us recall this important point: *angelos* (angel) means "messenger" in Greek and can at times refer to human beings (as in Lk 9:52).

[125] Already in Acts 10:25–26, we see Peter refuse the *proskynesis* Cornelius wishes to render him.

[126] See Mt 28:1–8; Mk 16:5; Lk 24:4–5.

medieval commentaries on Revelation that highlight this point very well:

So why does the angel so vehemently forbid [John to adore him], saying, "Do it not"? Because God was made man and took on a true human nature, which, having handed it over to passion and death for the whole world, he raised up and placed at the Father's right hand, and because he gave men, now his brethren and friends, the Holy Spirit of reconciliation, the dignity of human nature has grown beyond itself and has been brought to the measure of angelic dignity.[127]

But when angelic dignity, which did not forbid itself to be adored by man in the Old Testament, saw the God-Man raised up above itself in the New, it endured not to be adored by man.[128]

GOD'S GAZE IN THE NEW COVENANT

In the previous chapters, we spoke of the Creator's way of looking at his spiritual creatures (in our philosophical reflection on adoration) and God's way of looking at us as the Old Testament speaks of it. What do we find on this point in the New Testament?

In the New Covenant, the Father makes human beings His adoptive sons and daughters in Christ:

Blessed be the God and Father of our Lord Jesus Christ, who has blessed us in Christ with every spiritual blessing in the Heavenly places, even as he chose us in him before the foundation of the world, that we should be holy and blameless before him. He destined us in love to be his sons through Jesus Christ, according to the purpose of his will, to the praise of his glorious grace which he freely bestowed on us in the Beloved.[129]

---

[127] Rupert of Deutz, *Commentaria in Apocalypsim*, PL 169, 1161.
[128] Richard of St. Victor, *In Apocalypsim Joannis*, PL 196, 849.
[129] Eph 1:3–6.

By his Christian vocation, the disciple of Christ becomes a "son in the only Son"; he is called to live all that the Son lives. From that moment, the Father's gaze on the Christian could be nothing other than an extension of his gaze on Christ. The Gospels speak to us of this way of seeing, in particular in the episode of the baptism of Jesus in the Jordan River:

> *In those days Jesus came from Nazareth of Galilee and was baptized by John in the Jordan. And when he came up out of the water, immediately he saw the Heavens opened and the Spirit descending upon him like a dove; and a voice came from Heaven, "You are my beloved Son; with you I am well pleased."*[130]

In Luke's version of the baptism, the heavenly voice declares, "You are my beloved Son, today I have begotten thee," which is a quotation from Psalm 2.[131]

These words from the Father are addressed to Jesus. He is indeed the Father's beloved Son, the one whom the Father begets from all eternity and in whom he is well pleased. However, to the extent that our Christian vocation associates us with Christ to make us really share his life, the Father's look of love on Jesus extends to all his brethren. Therefore, each of us can hear in faith our Father say to us, "You are my beloved child, whom I beget to my divine life and in whom I am well pleased."[132]

CHRIST'S GAZE IN THE BOOK OF REVELATION

After seeing the way the Father looks at us according to the Gospels, let us turn to Christ's gaze. A beautiful New Tes-

---

[130] Mk 1:9–11.

[131] Lk 3:22, alternate reading; see Ps 2:7.

[132] It goes without saying that the good pleasure that the Father takes in us does not exempt us in any way from purifying ourselves from everything in us that still displeases God (sin). Quite the contrary.

tament text speaks to us about this gaze: the inaugural vision of Christ by John in Revelation 1:

> *Then I turned to see the voice that was speaking to me, and on turning I saw seven golden lampstands, and in the midst of the lampstands one like a son of man, clothed with a long robe and with a golden girdle round his breast; his head and his hair were white as white wool, white as snow; his eyes were like a flame of fire, his feet were like burnished bronze, refined as in a furnace, and his voice was like the sound of many waters; in his right hand he held seven stars, from his mouth issued a sharp two-edged sword, and his face was like the sun shining in full strength.*[133]

This passage contains the only physical description of Christ found in the New Testament, which indicates its great importance. However, it is not a corporeal description (as he died before the age of forty, Jesus certainly did not have white hair at the moment of his death), but rather a *theological description.* Its intention is not to satisfy our curiosity over the Christ's physical appearance, the color of his eyes and so on, but to transmit to us a teaching on what he is and on his mission. Without commenting on each of the symbolic traits of this description, let us pay attention to what John says of Christ's eyes: "his eyes were like a flame of fire, . . . and his face was like the sun shining in full strength." This is the way Christ looks at us; his look is a look of fire, just the opposite of a look of indifference. "God is love" (1 Jn 4:8, 16), and he does not change. Christ looks upon us with the greatest intensity of love, an intensity that we can hardly imagine, and it does not change. His look of love is certainly demanding; it is also the look of one "who searches mind and heart" (Rev 2:23). He comes to purify his Church, symbolized by the seven churches of Asia, with the fire of love; this is the

---

[133] Rev 1:12–16.

reason he is also represented as a smith ("his feet were like burnished bronze, refined as in a furnace"), for the smith works metals with fire to purify them.

Before the unique intensity of Christ's gaze, we understand John's instinctive reaction: "When I saw him, I fell at his feet as though dead" (Rev 1:17a). This is the reaction of one who is "floored" by the glory of God manifested to him. Could we not also say that this is a reaction of adoration? The verb *proskyneō* is not used here, but the instinctive action of falling to the ground suggests it.

Chapter 4: Theological Reflection on Adoration

After a philosophical analysis and a biblical exploration of adoration, let us now attempt to take up the question of adoration from a properly theological perspective.

To begin with, it is good to recall the great principle of the theology of grace: grace does not destroy human nature but assumes it, raises it up, and perfects it. Adoration has a natural foundation, and in this sense we can speak of *religious adoration*.

Because adoration preserves its natural foundation, it remains something demanded of the human being before God. Of course, we have become God's children through Christ; however, this does not do away with the fundamental fact, which we must never forget, that we remain God's creatures. In other words, we share God's *life* (imperfectly on earth by faith, and perfectly in Heaven), but we are *not* God. Our relationship with God is meant to be a filial one, in Christ, but it must also take on an attitude of adoration. We cannot fully be in the truth of our being before God if we do not adore him.[134] In this respect, the important place of adoration in the Book of Revelation is

[134] "God desires to communicate to us his friendship and intimacy, but he can do so only if we are open to him in a fair, true attitude. Before the Entirely Other, man must acknowledge his littleness, misery, and nothingness. Remember what Jesus said to Saint Catherine of Siena: 'I am the one who is; you are the one who is not.' Without radical humility that is expressed in gestures of adoration and in sacred rituals, no friendship with God is possible" (Cardinal Robert Sarah, *The Power of Silence*, 225–226, p. 120).

revealing: The saints in Heaven are God's children,[135] and yet they still adore him. These two dimensions of their relationship with God are fully lived in unity and harmony. The obligation to adore Christ remains as well, for he is God. Our relationship with Christ involves two dimensions: Christ is our friend, brother, bridegroom, and teacher, but he is also our God.[136] Moreover, it is significant that he too is adored, already on earth,[137] and then in Heaven under the figure of the Lamb, equally with the Father who sits on the throne:

> *And I heard every creature in Heaven and on earth and under the earth and in the sea, and all therein, saying, "To him who sits upon the throne and to the Lamb be blessing and honor and glory and might forever and ever!" And the four living creatures said, "Amen!" and the elders fell down and worshiped.*[138]

The Book of Revelation shows us Christ, on the one hand adoring the Father and presiding over heavenly adoration (under the symbolism of the four living beings in Revelation 4), and on the other hand, the object of human and angelic adoration (under the symbolism of the Lamb in Revelation 5).

CHRISTIAN ADORATION

For the Christian, adoration is raised up by divine grace in such a way as to become *properly Christian adoration.* It can be said that Christian adoration is the adoration in spirit and truth Christ came to teach on earth, the ado-

---

[135] "He who conquers shall have this heritage, and I will be his God and he shall be my son" (Rev 21:7).

[136] Christ is our friend (Jn 15:15), brother (Jn 20:17; Rm 8:29; Heb 2:11–12), bridegroom (Rev 19:7), teacher (Jn 13:13) and God (Jn 20:28).

[137] See Mt 14:33; Jn 9:38.

[138] Rev 5:13–14.

ration he himself lives fully, and of which he is the model:

> *It is an act of adoration as Christ himself performs it toward his beloved Father. Jesus performs this act in the depths of his human heart transformed by the fullness of his sanctifying grace as the Father's beloved Son.* . . .
> *Created charity informs all the acts of the infused virtues of Jesus' soul, and in the first place his acts of adoration, the exercise of his infused virtue of religion in adoration. In Jesus' soul, the acts of adoration are perfect, "in spirit and truth."*[139]

Some may find it odd that Jesus adores the Father. Is Christ not God in person? Can God adore God? What sense is there in that? In fact, we must be specific and say that although Jesus of Nazareth and the Word of God are indeed the same Person—this is the mystery of the hypostatic union—adoration is a personal act *according to a specific nature*, the human nature. The Word of God does not adore the Father according to his divine nature, since according to this nature he is equal to the Father, but he adores him according to his human nature, since he is truly man.

Now let us try to identify the specific characteristics of Christian adoration.

Adoration is a spiritual act, as we have seen. It is not necessarily bound to a particular place. Man can adore God wherever he may be. However, we should add that a "spiritual act" does not mean a disincarnated act. It is good for the body to be an active part of the act of adoration, as we saw earlier in the case of the adoration of the twenty-four elders prostrating themselves before God's throne. There are bodily attitudes that unquestionably favor adoration, while others make it more difficult. For example, it

---

[139] Marie-Dominique Philippe, "*Le Mystère de l'adoration*," in *Aletheia* 12 (*L'Adoration*), pp. 34–35.

is clear that it is not easy to adore the Lord deeply while relaxing in the sun in a rocking chair. On the other hand, actually kneeling, and even prostrating ourselves, helps us adore. In this regard, we should surely look carefully at Muslims. They have no fear of bowing down to the ground several times a day to adore God, even in places where they may be seen. It is certainly regrettable that the attitude of prostration is so rare among Christians.[140] It would be good to rediscover the biblical (and anthropological) roots of this bodily attitude in prayer.

Furthermore, the Christian's adoration is to be done "in truth." In the Gospel of John, the word "truth" has to do with the fullness of divine revelation brought by Christ.[141] The Christian must adore God in an attitude enlightened and shaped by Christian faith. Christians have received the grace of faith, which enables them, if they are faithful to it and let it grow within them, to know God more than non-Christians, including Muslims. This does not mean that Christians always adore God more and better than Muslims (sometimes the opposite is true), but it does mean that they have received a grace, which is at once a call and a mission, that *should* enable them to adore God more deeply.

In addition, although adoration has a natural foundation, Christian adoration goes beyond man's natural love for the Creator, because it is taken up by charity, divine love. He whom we adore bestows on us the immense grace of his divine friendship.[142]

---

[140] Some Christians even reject it as an attitude proper to Muslims! Such people seem not to have read Revelation 4. When he asks himself whether adoration, which is a properly spiritual act, also requires a bodily gesture, St. Thomas Aquinas responds in the affirmative: by genuflection, we confess our infirmity before God and by prostration we confess that we are nothing by ourselves before God (see *Summa Theologiae*, IIa-IIae, q. 84, a. 2, ad 2um).

[141] On this point, I refer to the masterful work by Ignace de la Potterie, *La Vérité dans saint Jean*.

[142] On charity as friendship with God, see: *Les Vertus théologales*, pp. 94–96.

So there is a Christian adoration, which like all authentic adoration, is rooted in natural adoration but which goes beyond it by faith and charity.[143]

This Christian adoration also has an essential connection with the Holy Spirit: We adore under the motion of the Holy Spirit. This point merits deeper consideration.

THE HOLY SPIRIT AND ADORATION

We have seen how adoration in spirit, which Jesus taught the Samaritan woman, could also be understood as "adoration in the [Holy] Spirit." What is the Holy Spirit's role in Christian adoration? It can be said that the Holy Spirit leads us so we may adore more and adore more deeply.

He does this by exercising the *gift of fear* within us, one of the seven gifts of the Holy Spirit.[144] When the Holy Spirit exercises this gift within us, the gift of fear gives us a respectful and reverent fear of God. We acknowledge that God in his infinite majesty is completely beyond us, and we pay him homage by adoration. The gift of fear inspires in us, not the fear of being punished by God (the "fear of the policeman"), but a holy fear, inspired by charity, of offending him by sin, of displeasing him and thus of distancing ourselves from him. By the exercise of the gift of fear, the Holy Spirit moves us to entrust ourselves to God, to rely on him and so, finally, to adore him. There is a close connection between the gift of fear and adoration. The gift of fear greatly helps us adore more frequently and more deeply than if we were to do so alone.

---

[143] Of course, Muslims of good faith can indeed receive spiritual assistance from God to help them live adoration more profoundly, even if they find themselves in a concrete situation that makes adherence to Christ difficult, or even impossible.

[144] On the gifts of the Holy Spirit, see: *Les Vertus théologales*, pp. 134–147.

In the act of Christian adoration, the Holy Spirit also helps us through the exercise of the *gift of piety*, which gives a filial note to our adoration of the Father:

> *But when the time had fully come, God sent forth his Son, born of woman, born under the law, to redeem those who were under the law, so that we might receive adoption as sons. And because you are sons, God has sent the Spirit of his Son into our hearts, crying, "Abba! Father!"* [145]

> *For all who are led by the Spirit of God are sons of God. For you did not receive the spirit of slavery to fall back into fear, but you have received the spirit of sonship. When we cry, "Abba! Father!" it is the Spirit himself bearing witness with our spirit that we are children of God."* [146]

This is perhaps where we best see the *Trinitarian dimension* of Christian adoration: we adore the Father with Jesus under the motion of the Holy Spirit; the Spirit puts Jesus' filial love for the Father into our hearts so that this love may become our own love and we may adore the Father as Jesus himself adores him.

To the extent that we entrust ourselves to God through the act of adoration, we allow the Holy Spirit to act on us and lead us further on in the divine life. To take up the human comparison of the mother and child once again, it is easier for a mother to care for a calm child who trustfully surrenders itself to her than to a turbulent child who constantly resists her. If we desire the Holy Spirit to take us far into divine life and enable us to taste more of God's goodness through the gift of wisdom, then it is of the utmost importance to adore. We must not deceive ourselves: A Christian who adores little or not at all will find it difficult to be docile to the Holy Spirit.

---

[145] Gal 4:4–6.
[146] Rom 8:14–16.

LIVING BY ADORATION

Let us look at a few aspects of the way to live by adoration in the Christian life.

Understanding the importance of adoration in the Christian life also means understanding that our adoration must be fervent. Since Christian adoration is taken up by charity, we can say about the fervor of adoration what has been said about charity:[147] adoration is fervent when it is intense and when it is frequent.

Adoration is meant to take hold of the human heart to its very depths, according to the exhortation of the *Shema Israel*: "You shall love the Lord your God with all your heart, and with all your soul, and with all your might" (Dt 6:4). In order for the whole person to be seized by adoration, it is good, if possible, to associate the body with it through the biblical gesture of prostration. However, when this is not possible, nothing prevents us from doing the inner act of adoration in our hearts, for it is not necessary to go to Jerusalem or Mount Gerizim, or even to a church, to adore.

We saw earlier that adoration is lived so well in Heaven that "day and night they never cease" (Rev 4:8). We are not in Heaven; we cannot yet live unceasing adoration, but it is desirable for our days to be punctuated by frequent acts of adoration taking us ever closer to heavenly adoration. Adoration of the Blessed Sacrament, which we will look at later on, can be an excellent means of plunging into adoration of the Lord, but adoration must not be restricted to times of adoring the Blessed Sacrament.

---

[147] See *Les Vertus théologales*, pp. 100–101.

THE FRUITS OF ADORATION

Let us consider the fruits that adoration produces in the Christian life when practiced habitually.

DOCILITY TO THE HOLY SPIRIT. Among the fruits that adoration produces in our lives is one we have just mentioned: docility to the Holy Spirit. This docility is of the greatest importance for the Holy Spirit to be able to make us progress toward holiness: "All who are led by the Spirit of God are sons of God" (Rom 8: 14). The Holy Spirit is very respectful of our freedom. He will lead us only if we accept to let ourselves be led by him, and this presupposes a great desire on our part to be moved by him and a great docility toward him. To the extent that adoration makes us entrust ourselves to God, it greatly favors docility to the Holy Spirit, without which we cannot move forward in the spiritual life.

PEACE AND SURRENDER. Adoration also begets inner peace. When we are tossed to and fro by the trials of life, or even prey to anguish in the face of grave danger, adoration reminds us that we are not alone and that we are in God's hands. Nothing that happens to us escapes God's Providence. Although we may be caught up from time to time in the storms of life, God does not change; he still carries us in his fatherly love. Adoration leads us to surrender to God and his Providence, sure that he is watching over us. This abandonment flows from our theological life; it is not a psychological abandonment consisting in doing nothing. We are to assume our human and Christian responsibilities and do what we must as well as we can. However, adoration reminds us that our lives are in God's hands and moves us to entrust ourselves to him in the assurance of his love. In this sense, adoration keeps us in hope:

> *Only the great certitude of hope that my own life and history in general, despite all failures, are held firm by the indestructible power of Love, and that this gives them their meaning and importance, only this kind of hope can then give the courage to act and to persevere.*[148]

Clearly, given the fragilities of human nature, adoration does not do away with the necessity for some to turn to doctors and psychologists, or even psychiatrists, but adoration is an important factor for attaining inner peace. Let us consider St. Teresa of Avila's beautiful prayer:

> *Let nothing trouble you,*
> *Nothing frighten you.*
> *All is passing.*
> *God changes not.*
> *Patience obtains all.*
> *One who has God*
> *Lacks nothing.*
> *God alone is enough.*

INNER SILENCE. Adoration creates in our hearts the inner silence by which we can be increasingly present to the one who dwells by his grace in the inmost depths of our souls. We too often forget God's loving presence within us because too often we live at the surface of ourselves. Mother Teresa of Calcutta liked to say, "God speaks in the silence, and we listen." This discretion and gentleness of God are already illustrated in the Old Testament by the lovely episode of the prophet Elijah's meeting with the Lord on Mount Horeb (or Sinai):

---

[148] Benedict XVI, Encyclical Letter *Spe Salvi* 35.

And [God] said, "Go forth, and stand upon the mount before the Lord." And behold, the Lord passed by, and a great and strong wind rent the mountains, and broke in pieces the rocks before the Lord, but the Lord was not in the wind; and after the wind an earthquake, but the Lord was not in the earthquake; and after the earthquake a fire, but the Lord was not in the fire; and after the fire a still small voice. And when Elijah heard it, he wrapped his face in his mantle and went out and stood at the entrance of the cave. And behold, there came a voice to him, and said, "What are you doing here, Elijah?"[149]

The Lord was not present in extraordinary phenomena that strike the human imagination but in a small voice, which could be translated even more literally as "like the voice of a light silence" (*kol demamah daqah*).

To have a profound prayer life, we definitely need a minimum of outward silence during our prayer times. Experience shows, however, that outward silence is not enough, for our souls are noisy at times, and so we have trouble meeting up with the Lord and listening to his voice. One of the effects of adoration, when it is practiced frequently, is to engender inner silence in the soul. The importance of adoration for our prayer life was highlighted by John Paul II:

> *The Christians of the East turn to God as Father, Son and Holy Spirit, living persons tenderly present, to whom they utter a solemn and humble, majestic and simple liturgical doxology. But they perceive that one draws close to this presence above all by letting oneself be taught an adoring silence, for at the culmination of the knowledge and experience of God is his absolute transcendence. This is reached through the prayerful assimilation of Scripture and the liturgy more than by systematic meditation.*
>
> *In the humble acceptance of the creature's limits before the infinite transcendence of a God who never ceases to reveal himself as God-Love, the Father of our Lord Jesus Christ in the joy of*

---

[149] 2 Kgs 19:11–13.

the Holy Spirit, I see expressed the attitude of prayer and the theological method which the East prefers and continues to offer all believers in Christ.

We must confess that we all have need of this silence, filled with the presence of him who is adored: in theology, so as to exploit fully its own sapiential and spiritual soul; in prayer, so that we may never forget that seeing God means coming down the mountain with a face so radiant that we are obliged to cover it with a veil (cf. Ex 34:33), and that our gatherings may make room for God's presence and avoid self-celebration; in preaching, so as not to delude ourselves that it is enough to heap word upon word to attract people to the experience of God; in commitment, so that we will refuse to be locked in a struggle without love and forgiveness.[150]

HUMILITY.   Let us mention another fruit of adoration in us: humility. We have a great deal of trouble becoming humble. Pride is the main defect, the most serious and hidden defect, in each of us. The reason for this is a simple one: The original sin, whose consequences we have inherited, was a sin of pride, the attempt to become God on our own. Naturally, we can have other more visible faults (such as gluttony, impatience, and so on), but pride is always our main fault. It is our gravest fault because it is what most opposes God's love in us. Without God's grace, we can hardly begin to become humble, and we even have great difficulty understanding just how proud we are. In his mercy, the Lord enlightens and purifies us by his grace. However, as always when it comes to our sanctification, our cooperation is required.[151] What is the best cooperation we can offer God to become humble? Adoration. Adoration gives us a lively sense of

---

[150] John Paul II, Apostolic Letter *Orientale Lumen* 16. Cardinal Sarah makes the same point with different words: "Sacred silence, laden with adored presence, opens the way to mystical silence, full of loving intimacy" (*The Power of Silence*, 232, p. 122).

[151] "God created us without us, but has not willed to save us without us" (St. Augustine, Sermon 169, 11, 13).

who God is—the Creator—and what we are—creatures totally dependent on the Creator. The deeper the grasp we have of this sense, the more we desire to exalt God rather than ourselves. All the saints give us examples of humility, naturally, but we find a particularly amazing clarity on the subject of pride, both for its depth and for its precocity (since she was but seventeen at the time), in St. Teresa of the Andes:

> *And to think that the root of all sin is pride, which is my dominant passion. . . .*
>   *What do I have, Lord, that You haven't given me?. . .*
>   *I have understood that what most keeps me from God is my pride. From now on, I desire and propose to be humble. Without humility, the rest of the virtues are hypocrisy. Without that, the graces received from God are harmful and ruinous. Humility brings us the likeness of Christ, peace of soul, holiness and intimate union with God.*[152]

DETACHMENT FROM IDOLS.   Let us mention yet another beneficial effect of adoration in the Christian life: It contributes to the detachment of our hearts from idols and attaches them to God alone. The temptation of idolatry is not just a thing of the past, of Old Testament times. It is an ever-recurrent temptation in the history of humanity, to the extent that the human heart, wounded by the consequences of original sin, still has a disordered tendency to adore idols. In this regard, we might be tempted to borrow the words of Mephistopheles in the famous ballad *"Le Veau d'or est toujours debout"* from Gounod's opera *Faust*:

> *The calf of gold is still standing!*
> *One adulates his power.*
> *From one end of the world to the other!*

---

[152] St. Teresa of the Andes, "Diary" 29, pp. 237–238.

> *To celebrate the infamous idol,*
> *Kings and people mixed together,*
> *To the somber sound of golden coins,*
> *They dance a wild round*
> *Around his pedestal.*
> *And Satan leads the dance.*[153]

If there is a risk of idolatry at the collective level, there is also risk of idolatry at the personal level, the danger of putting ourselves first always and in everything. We must keep unbolting from the pedestal of our hearts the statue of ourselves that we always tend to create so as to adore but God alone. Let us listen to Teresa of the Andes once more:

> *We'll ask Jesus at Communion that He build in our souls a little house; that we will provide the building material, which will be our efforts at humbling and forgetting ourselves, at doing away with our egos, for these are the idols we adore interiorly. This is hard and will bring cries of pain from us. But Jesus asks for that throne and we must give it to Him. Charity will be the weapon to overcome those idols.*[154]

OBEDIENCE.   In the act of adoration, we make the spiritual offering to God of what we are, which comes from him, and therefore in particular of our personal will. We put ourselves in God's hands. From that moment, we dispose ourselves to greater acceptance and fulfillment of the Father's will for us. Adoration thus helps us obey God's will.

In this respect, it is interesting to note that right after the dialogue with the Samaritan woman, Jesus declares, "My food is to do the will of him who sent me, and to accomplish his work" (Jn 4:34).

---

[153] Charles Gounod, *Faust* libretto, trans. Lea Frey—from www.aria-database.com/translations/faust.txt (September 2013).

[154] Letter 8, of 15 April 1916, to her sister Rebecca, p. 13.

Adoration also disposes us to accept painful trials. In the Old Testament, Job is a good witness to this truth. After he heard the terrible news of his children's death, the massacre of his servants and the loss of his flock, Job reacts admirably with an act of adoration that enables him to bear this trial without revolting against God: "Then Job arose, and rent his robe, and shaved his head, and fell upon the ground, and worshiped" (Job 1:20).

ADORATION AND LITURGY

Adoration has a role to play not only in one's personal life, but also in the life of the community, particularly in the liturgy. We have seen in the Book of Revelation that the vision of adoration in Heaven (Rev 4) preceded that of the heavenly liturgy (Rev 5). This order is significant: adoration must precede and envelop the earthly liturgy, which is meant to be in unison with the heavenly liturgy.

On this subject, we can say that several dangers threaten the exercise of liturgy. There is the danger of *vulgarity* (common songs, common vestments and furnishings, disrespectful attire), which offends the dignity of liturgy. There is the danger of *performance* (either because liturgy becomes a show or because the pursuit of the aesthetic takes precedence), in which we forget that we are in the presence of the mystery of God giving himself to us. Inversely, there is the danger of *formalism* and ritualism in which one settles for merely mechanical, literal observance of the rubrics of the liturgical books. Christian liturgy must be lived in adoration to be fully operative, that is, to raise men up to God and introduce them into his mystery. Adoration spontaneously gives us the sense of respect for God's presence and for liturgical actions. It creates a climate favorable to interiorizing what happens in liturgy in such a way that liturgy can produce all its spiritual fruit. A

Cistercian abbot, Dom Belorgey, told the story of how his monastery had been deeply renewed in liturgical prayer through each monk's greater commitment to adoration. The monks of this monastery had been so absorbed by their work that the quality of the Divine Office suffered. When he was elected abbot of the monastery, Dom Belorgey reminded each monk in particular and the community as a whole of the importance of adoration in monastic life. He exhorted his community to a renewal of adoration. After a few months, the monastery had regained a deeply contemplative atmosphere.[155]

ADORATION IN THE LIFE OF ELIZABETH OF THE TRINITY

Clearly, all the saints lived adoration in spirit and truth; nonetheless, it is true that some lived it in a particularly eminent way. This is undoubtedly the case with St. Elizabeth of the Trinity (1880-1906). It is striking to see how frequently she uses words connected to adoration. It would be difficult to find many saints who had as profound a sense of adoration as Elizabeth.[156] For this reason, I would like to cite three passages from Elizabeth about adoration.

Jesus Christ, the True Adorer in Spirit and Truth: The first passage is a brief meditation on Jesus' teaching to the Samaritan woman:

> *Christ said one day to the Samaritan woman that "the Father seeks true adorers in spirit and truth." To give joy to His Heart, let us be these true adorers. Let us adore Him in "spirit," that is, with our hearts and our thoughts fixed on Him, and our mind filled with His knowledge imparted by the light of faith. Let us adore Him in "truth," that is, by our works, for it is above all by our*

---

[155] This story is told in greater detail in Marie-Dominique Philippe, *Wherever He Goes*, pp. 22–23.

[156] Outside of adoration of the Blessed Sacrament.

actions that we show we are true: this is to do always what is pleasing to the Father whose children we are. And finally, let us "adore in spirit and in truth," that is through Jesus Christ and with Jesus Christ, for He alone is the true Adorer in spirit and truth.[157]

This short paragraph is a summary of the essence of Christian adoration.

O My God, Trinity Whom I Adore: The second passage is her well-known prayer to the Blessed Trinity:

O my God, Trinity whom I adore, help me to forget myself entirely that I may be established in You as still and as peaceful as if my soul were already in eternity. May nothing trouble my peace or make me leave You, O my Unchanging One, but may each minute carry me further into the depths of Your Mystery. Give peace to my soul; make it Your Heaven, Your beloved dwelling and Your resting place. May I never leave You there alone but be wholly present, my faith wholly vigilant, wholly adoring, and wholly surrendered to Your creative Action.

O My beloved Christ, crucified by love, I wish to be a bride for Your Heart: I wish to cover You with glory; I wish to love You . . . even unto death! But I feel my weakness, and I ask You to "clothe me with Yourself," to identify my soul with all the movements of Your Soul, to overwhelm me, to possess me, to substitute Yourself for me that my life may be but a radiance of Your life. Come into me as Adorer, as Restorer, as Savior. O Eternal Word, Word of my God, I want to spend my life in listening to You, to become wholly teachable that I may learn all from You. Then, through all nights, all voids, all helplessness, I want to gaze on You always and remain in Your great light. O my beloved Star, so fascinate me that I may not withdraw from Your radiance.

O consuming Fire, Spirit of Love, "come upon me," and create in my soul a kind of incarnation of the Word: that I may be another

---

[157] Elizabeth of the Trinity, "Heaven in Faith" 33, *I Have Found God*, vol. I, p. 108.

humanity for Him in which He can renew His whole Mystery. And You, O Father, bend lovingly over Your poor little creature; "cover her with Your shadow," seeing in her only the "Beloved in whom You are well pleased."

O my Three, my All, my Beatitude, infinite Solitude, Immensity in which I lose myself, I surrender myself to You as Your prey. Bury Yourself in me that I may bury myself in You until I depart to contemplate in Your light the abyss of Your greatness.[158]

Without going into a detailed commentary on this prayer here, let us simply bring out the place adoration has in it.

First, Elizabeth starts right off with an act of adoration: "O my God, Trinity whom I adore." She cannot put herself in God's presence without immediately adoring him. This adoration takes hold of her entirely and is experienced as a loving response to God's creative action: "May I . . . be wholly present, my faith wholly vigilant, wholly adoring, and wholly surrendered to Your creative Action."

Elizabeth then addresses Christ, expressing to him her desire to be mystically identified with him so as to share his life fully, and the first aspect of Christ's life she mentions is adoration: "Come into me as Adorer, as Restorer, as Savior." Elizabeth therefore ardently desires for her adoration to be an extension within her soul of Christ's adoration of the Father. She wants to adore through him, with him and in him.

Adoration Is a Word from Heaven: The third passage, less well-known than the two previous passages, is drawn from the meditations of Elizabeth's last retreat, a few weeks before her death. It is a meditation on Revelation 4, which we

---

[158] Elizabeth of the Trinity, "O My God, Trinity Whom I Adore," *I Have Found God*, vol. I, pp. 183–184.

studied earlier, having to do with heavenly adoration. I quote this magnificent text in its entirety, adding a few clarifications in brackets:

> *"They [the twenty-four elders] fall down and adore, they cast down their crowns. . . ." First of all the soul should "fall down," should plunge into the abyss of its nothingness, sinking so deeply into it that in the beautiful expression of a mystic [the Fleming Ruysbroeck], it finds "true, unchanging, and perfect peace which no one can disturb, for it has plunged so low that no one will look for it there."*
>
> *Then it can "adore." Adoration, ah! That is a word from Heaven! It seems to me it can be defined as the ecstasy of love. It is love overcome by the beauty, the strength, the immense grandeur of the Object loved, and it "falls down in a kind of faint" in an utterly profound silence, that silence of which David spoke when he exclaimed: "Silence is Your praise!" Yes, this is the most beautiful praise since it is sung eternally in the bosom of the tranquil Trinity; and it is also the "last effort of the soul that overflows and can say no more. . . ." [Lacordaire].*
>
> *"Adore the Lord, for He is holy," the Psalmist says. And again: "They will adore Him always because of Himself." The soul that is absorbed in recollection of these thoughts, that penetrates them with "this mind of God" of which St. Paul speaks, lives in an anticipated Heaven, beyond all that passes, beyond the clouds, beyond itself! It knows that He whom it adores possesses in Himself all happiness and all glory and, "casting its crown" before Him as the blessed do, it despises self, loses sight of self, and finds its beatitude in that of the adored Being, in the midst of every suffering and sorrow. For it has left self, it has "passed" into Another. It seems to me that in this attitude of adoration the soul "resembles those wells" of which St. John of the Cross speaks, which receive "the waters that flow down from Lebanon," and we can say on seeing it: "The impetus of the river delights the City of God" [Ps 46(45):5].*[159]

For Elizabeth, to live adoration is already to live the life of Heaven, for the life of the blessed in Heaven is a life of

---

[159] Ibid., "Last Retreat" 21, pp. 150–151.

adoration; this is indeed what Revelation 4 shows us. Adoration is first a love, an ecstatic love making man go out of himself to love God, who is infinitely beyond him and whose greatness and holiness cause him to faint, as it were. It begets silence in the adoring soul and leads the soul to "despise itself" (in the sense that it favors the attitude of humility before God).

To the extent that it lives in adoration, the soul goes further and further beyond all earthly contingencies, including the inevitable trials and sufferings of human life; its life is more and more God's own life; in him it finds its beatitude, already on this earth, as it waits to share in it fully in Heaven. It opens up more and more to God, who is able to fill it with his gifts, hence the comparison of the soul to a well of living water.

In passing, let us note in this text some of the effects of adoration that we have mentioned above: peace and silence.

THE GLANCE OF CHRIST IN THE WRITINGS
OF THÉRÈSE OF LISIEUX

Earlier we saw texts of Scripture that spoke to us of God's gaze on human beings and of Christ's gaze on John. Let us conclude this chapter by quoting some beautiful texts of St. Thérèse of the Child Jesus about God's gaze, especially in connection with the Holy Face, and by seeing how the contemplation of Jesus' face awakens adoration within her. We find in the Little Thérèse a veritable fascination with the mystery of the Face of Christ.[160] Here is one portion of the Act of Oblation to Merciful Love on this subject:

[O my God,] Since You loved me so much as to give me your only Son as my Savior and my Spouse, the infinite

---

[160] Let us recall that she had chosen to be called Thérèse of the Child Jesus and the Holy Face.

treasures of his merits are mine. I offer them to you with gladness, begging you to look on me only through the Face of Jesus and in his Heart burning with Love.

I want to console you for the ingratitude of the wicked, and I beg of you to take away my freedom to displease you. If through weakness I sometimes fall, may your Divine Glance cleanse my soul immediately, consuming all my imperfections like the fire that transforms everything into itself.[161]

Thérèse understands that it is through His Son that the Father looks at us. This look is merciful, for we are poor sinners. Far from fearing God's glance (like Adam and Eve trying to hide from God after their sin in the Garden of Eden), Thérèse seeks and desires it, since she knows God's desire is to cleanse us of all our impurities. This is a teaching similar to that of the Book of Revelation, in the inaugural vision of chapter 1: Christ's gaze is a fiery flame purifying the churches.

Here are other texts of Thérèse's prayers and poems:

> *I ask you, O my God: not to look at what I am but what I should be and want to be, a religious wholly inflamed with your love.*
>
> *O Adorable Face of Jesus, the only Beauty that captivates my heart, deign to imprint in me your Divine Likeness so that you may not behold the soul of your little bride without seeing Yourself in her.* [162]

> *O my Beloved, for love of you, I accept not seeing here below the gentleness of your Look nor feeling the ineffable kiss of your Mouth, but I beg you to inflame me with your love so that it may consume me rapidly and soon bring me into your presence.*[163]

---

[161] St. Thérèse of the Child Jesus, "Act of Oblation to Merciful Love," pp. 53–54.

[162] "Prayer 8: Prayer for Abbé Bellière", in *The Prayers of Saint Thérèse of Lisieux*, p. 78.

[163] "Prayer 16: To the Holy Face," in ibid., p. 104.

Thérèse is delighted before the face of Jesus. The excessive love for humanity expressed in the Holy Face of the Man of Sorrows awakens adoration in her. Thérèse accepts to live Jesus' look of love on her in faith, without tasting its ineffable sweetness.

> *Your Son's ineffable glance*
> *Has deigned to lower itself to my poor soul.*
> *I have searched for his adorable Face,*
> *And in Him I want to hide myself.*
> *I will always have to stay little*
> *To be worthy of his glances,*
> *But I'll grow quickly in virtue*
> *Under the brightness of this star of Heaven.*[164]

The contemplation of Christ's face is sanctifying. We cannot expose ourselves to Jesus' eyes for any length of time without being changed. Thérèse wishes to abide in this contemplation and thus grow quickly toward holiness. This contemplation is the foretaste of the clear vision of God's face in the beatific vision of Heaven:

> *To bear the exile of this valley of tears*
> *I need the glance of my Divine Savior.*
> *This glance full of love has revealed its charms to me.*
> *It has made me sense the happiness of Heaven.*
> *My Jesus smiles at me when I sigh to Him.*
> *Then I no longer feel my trial of faith.*
> *My God's Glance, his ravishing Smile,*
> *That is Heaven for me! . . .*[165]

---

[164] PN 11, *The Poetry of Saint Thérèse of Lisieux*, 73.
[165] PN 32, ibid., 153.

Chapter 5: Adoration of the Blessed Sacrament

In this chapter, I will say a few words on adoration of the Blessed Sacrament. This practice, which appeared in the Western Church during the Middle Ages, has greatly developed since that time, thanks especially to the institution of the feast of the Blessed Sacrament, Corpus Christi, at the instigation of St. Juliana of Mont Cornillon. After undergoing something of an eclipse in the years following the Second Vatican Council, it is being rediscovered today by many Christian individuals and prayer groups. Many parishes have even instituted perpetual Eucharistic adoration, which bears a great abundance of spiritual fruit.

Adoration of the Blessed Sacrament has always been warmly recommended by the Supreme Pontiffs. In this respect, let us look at what John Paul II wrote in his final encyclical, *Ecclesia de Eucharistia*:

> *The worship of the Eucharist outside of the Mass is of inestimable value for the life of the Church. This worship is strictly linked to the celebration of the Eucharistic Sacrifice. The presence of Christ under the sacred species reserved after Mass—a presence which lasts as long as the species of bread and of wine remain—derives from the celebration of the sacrifice and is directed toward communion, both sacramental and spiritual. . . .*
>
> *It is pleasant to spend time with him, to lie close to his breast like the Beloved Disciple (cf. Jn 13:25) and to feel the infinite love present in his heart. If in our time Christians must be distinguished above all by the "art of prayer," how can we not feel a renewed need to spend time in spiritual converse, in silent adora-*

tion, in heartfelt love before Christ present in the Most Holy Sacrament? . . .

This practice, repeatedly praised and recommended by the Magisterium, is supported by the example of many saints. Particularly outstanding in this regard was St. Alphonsus Liguori, who wrote: "Of all devotions, that of adoring Jesus in the Blessed Sacrament is the greatest after the sacraments, the one dearest to God and the one most helpful to us." The Eucharist is a priceless treasure: by not only celebrating it but also by praying before it outside of Mass we are enabled to make contact with the very wellspring of grace.[166]

Adoration of the Blessed Sacrament produces excellent fruit in the Christian life. Here we will look more particularly at the connection between the adoration of the Blessed Sacrament and Christian adoration in general, of which we have spoken up to this point, for as we have seen, adoration has a much greater extension than only adoration of the Blessed Sacrament.

REAL PRESENCE AND INDWELLING PRESENCE

The Church believes in the real presence of Christ in the Eucharist. What does "real presence" mean? Is Christ only truly present in the Eucharist? Here it is necessary to distinguish different types of God's presence:

—God is present to all his creatures, for he is the one who bears them in being. This is what we call God's "presence of immensity" in his creatures.

—God is particularly present in the persons who have sanctifying grace, according to this saying of Christ: "If a man loves me, he will keep my word, and my Father will love him, and we will come to him and make our home with him" (Jn 14:23). It is important to recall (for we often

---

[166] John Paul II, Encyclical *Ecclesia de Eucharistia* 25.

forget) that we bear this presence of God in us in the depths of our hearts. God is not far from us!

—Also, there is the unique case of Christ's presence in the Eucharist. This is what Pope Paul VI says about it:

> *This presence is called "real" not to exclude the idea that the others are "real" too, but rather to indicate presence par excellence, because it is substantial and through it Christ becomes present whole and entire, God and man.*[167]

It is by reason of the real, substantial presence of Christ in the Eucharist that it is fitting to adore the Blessed Sacrament. Christ is not present in the hearts of the faithful in a substantial way, which is why I do not genuflect before them as they pass by!

Some object that the Eucharist was instituted by Christ as something to be eaten. This is true, naturally. We must remember that, inasmuch as it is a sacrament, the Eucharist is a means of sanctification of the faithful during their life on earth, so they must use it by eating it. We can even say the following: Indeed, Christ's real presence in the Eucharist is more *perfect* than his indwelling presence in the hearts of the faithful; however, it is *finalized* by his indwelling presence. In other words, the goal of the reception of the Eucharist is to make the Lord's indwelling presence grow in us, for this presence is connected to sanctifying grace, which normally grows with the reception of the Eucharist.

It is therefore clear that adoration of the Blessed Sacrament ought not make us forget Eucharistic communion. However, it should be noted that this is rarely the case. It is good for there to be interplay between Eucharistic communion and adoration of the Blessed Sacrament; the one is to lead us to the other.

---

[167] Paul VI, Encyclical *Mysterium Fidei* (1965) 39.

In Pope Benedict XVI's apostolic exhortation on the Eucharist, he comes back to the previously mentioned objection:

> *For example, an objection that was widespread at the time argued that the Eucharistic bread was given to us not to be looked at, but to be eaten. In the light of the Church's experience of prayer, however, this was seen to be a false dichotomy. As St. Augustine put it: "nemo autem illam carnem manducat, nisi prius adoraverit; peccemus non adorando—no one eats that flesh without first adoring it; we should sin were we not to adore it." (191) In the Eucharist, the Son of God comes to meet us and desires to become one with us; Eucharistic adoration is simply the natural consequence of the Eucharistic celebration, which is itself the Church's supreme act of adoration.*[168]

CONTEMPLATING CHRIST'S LOVE IN THE EUCHARIST

What is the importance of adoration of the Blessed Sacrament? What specifically does it bring to Christian adoration, with which we have dealt throughout this book?

The Grace of the Real Presence.   First of all, the Eucharist gives us the wonderful gift of Christ's real presence. In Eucharistic communion we carry within us the Lord's real presence for as long as the Eucharistic species of the bread or wine remain, which is only a few minutes and no more. After that, the species are dissolved in our stomachs and the real presence disappears. This fact should lead us all the more to understand the importance of making the most of the moment after Holy Communion to be united to the Lord in a prayer of thanksgiving. In adoration of the Blessed Sacrament, on the other hand, the Lord's real

---

[168] Benedict XVI, Apostolic Exhortation *Sacramentum Caritatis* 66. The quotation from St. Augustine is taken from his commentary on Psalm 99(98).

presence remains right there before us. Is having the Blessed Sacrament necessary in order to pray, to the point that we could only pray with the Eucharistic real presence? Clearly not. We can pray practically anywhere. There are religious communities that practice perpetual Eucharistic adoration, but there are others, even ancient and venerable ones such as the Carthusians, in which members usually engage in silent interior prayer without the Eucharistic real presence. There is a legitimate diversity of spiritual traditions in this matter which must be respected. However, experience seems to show that it is easier to pray with the real presence than without it, whether the Blessed Sacrament is exposed in a monstrance on the altar or simply reposes in the tabernacle. How are we to understand this? The fact of the matter is that *Christ*, really present in the Eucharist, *is drawing us to himself*.

The Blessed Sacrament exerts an attraction on us, one that is hidden and mysterious but real. This is undoubtedly what explains why it is generally easier to concentrate in prayer with the real presence than without it. It seems that children and young people commonly have this experience in our day; they enter into prayer more easily in the presence of the Blessed Sacrament than in its absence.[169] The little Audrey Stevenson, who died in the odor of sanctity at eight years of age, is a lovely example of this. Audrey suffered from terminal leukemia. Because of their exceptional circumstances, her family had received from the bishop the rarely-granted permission to keep the Eucharistic presence in a room of their home they had set aside for this use and which had become the family "chapel." Audrey prayed there often. As summer began, they took her to another

---

[169] On Eucharistic adoration for children, see in particular the Children of Hope website, an association that promotes it in many countries of the world, especially in the United States: www.childrenofhope.org. It produces beautiful spiritual fruit.

house in Normandy. Audrey was happy to go. However, when she entered that house, she burst into tears. Her mother was taken by surprise and asked, "What's wrong, Audrey? Aren't you happy we've come to Maillot?" Between sobs, she answered, "Yes. But my Lord isn't here."[170] It had not been possible to bring the Eucharistic presence on vacation, and Audrey clearly felt the difference; she had the impression that the house was empty.

It seems clear that Christ's Eucharistic presence brings with it a particular grace making it easier to enter into prayer. In this regard, we can say that Eucharistic adoration is an excellent way to enter into adoration in spirit and truth.

The connection between adoration with and without Eucharistic adoration is made by Pope Benedict XVI in his closing homily for the World Youth Days in Cologne in 2005, whose theme was precisely "We have come to adore him":

The Greek word [for adoration] is "proskynesis." It refers to the gesture of submission, the recognition of God as our true measure, supplying the norm that we choose to follow. It means that freedom is not simply about enjoying life in total autonomy, but rather about living by the measure of truth and goodness, so that we ourselves can become true and good. This gesture is necessary even if initially our yearning for freedom makes us inclined to resist it.

We can only fully accept it when we take the second step that the Last Supper proposes to us. The Latin word for adoration is "adoratio"—mouth to mouth contact, a kiss, an embrace, and hence, ultimately love. Submission becomes union, because he to whom we submit is Love. In this way submission acquires a meaning, because it does not impose anything on us from the outside, but liberates us deep within.[171]

---

[170] Gloria Conde, *Audrey: The True Story of a Child's Heroic Journey of Faith*, p. 157.

[171] Benedict XVI, Homily for the closing Mass of the World Youth Days, Cologne, 21 August 2005.

Therefore, Eucharistic adoration helps us enter into a Christian life of adoration.

Adoring in Silence. Adoration of the Blessed Sacrament, especially nocturnal adoration, is most often done in silence, even if sometimes accompanied by liturgical chants. Staying in silence before Jesus for long periods can at times seem something of a trial, especially when we experience dryness in prayer. This outward silence is meant to help us reach inner silence, so that we can contemplate Christ's look of love on us and respond to this look with adoration:

> *The Holy Spirit leads us close to the Eucharist so that we might enter into the silence of adoration. The Eucharist should teach us to adore, and adoration is the first desert that God gives us. In adoration one is alone before God; it is the Holy Spirit's first education for us, so that we might discover more profoundly our bond of dependence with regard to God, Creator and Father—a loving dependence, a dependence that liberates us.*[172]

The Eucharist, Witness of Christ's Love for Us. All the saints have had immense love for the Eucharist, and many expressed this love in their writings. In this area, there are simply too many texts to choose from:

> *It seems to me that nothing better expresses the love in God's Heart than the Eucharist: it is union, consummation, He in us, we in Him, and isn't that Heaven on earth?*[173]

Once more we shall quote St. Teresa of the Andes. In her correspondence she speaks of the way that contemplation of Christ present in the Eucharist fills her with love:

---

[172] Marie-Dominique Philippe, *I Thirst: Conferences on the Wisdom of the Cross* 61.

[173] Elizabeth of the Trinity, Letter 165 to Abbé Chevignard, *Letters* 105.

The other day, coming before the exposition of the Most Blessed Sacrament, I was asking myself, why don't we all fall madly in love with Him? [174]

There [in the tabernacle], reduced to nothingness, He lives for His creatures' sake. Only the sanctuary lamp reveals His presence. What love, my dear Isabel! It is beyond understanding. I ask myself often why all of us don't go crazy with love for our God. [175]

What can He refuse you when He's on fire with love for you, since He has already reduced Himself to nothingness to come to you! [176]

God made Himself nourishment for His creatures. Have you ever thought deeply about the infinite madness of this love? Believe me, I feel my soul overwhelmed with gratitude and love. My life is spent contemplating that incomprehensible Goodness, and my soul suffers when I see that Love is unknown. I plunge myself deeply into His grandeur, into His wisdom. But when I think about His goodness, my heart is speechless. I adore Him. . . . [177]

Adoration Helps Us Receive the Eucharist Fruitfully. The Eucharist is worthy to be adored because in it Christ is really present. At the same time, adoration of the Blessed Sacrament helps us receive the Eucharist profitably by disposing us to receive the graces of the Sacrament fruitfully, in order to strengthen our personal bonds with the Lord and with our brothers and sisters:

Receiving the Eucharist means adoring him whom we receive. Only in this way do we become one with him, and are given, as it were, a foretaste of the beauty of the Heavenly liturgy. The act of adoration outside Mass prolongs and intensifies all that takes place

[174] Elizabeth of the Trinity, Letter 165 of 25 June 1918 to Mother Angelica Teresa, *Letters* 53.

[175] Letter 109 of 13 June 1919 to Elisa Valdes Ossa, *Letters* 250.

[176] Letter 114 of 12 July 1919 to her sister Rebeca, *Letters* 263.

[177] Letter 121 to Ines Salas Pereira, *Letters* 283.

during the liturgical celebration itself. Indeed, "only in adoration can a profound and genuine reception mature. And it is precisely this personal encounter with the Lord that then strengthens the social mission contained in the Eucharist, which seeks to break down not only the walls that separate the Lord and ourselves, but also and especially the walls that separate us from one another." [178]

The Eucharist Makes Us Enter Christ's Adoration.   If Christ is indeed the one who fully practices adoration in spirit and truth, at the Cross his adoration reaches perfection:

> *Adoration "in spirit and truth" is the hidden source of the bloody sacrifice of his [Jesus'] whole self on the Cross, and thereby adoration is what allows the Father's love to be victorious in silence, burning up all that is not love. By adoration, the Father's love is victorious over everything. This is why revelation terminates through the Cross and at the Cross by the cry of thirst, which incarnates adoration in an ultimate way. The primacy of love, of the desire to love, is thus revealed. It is truly through adoration that God can ultimately reveal himself in all his absoluteness: "I thirst!"* [179]

The Eucharist gives us the sacrifice of the Cross substantially. It gives it to us sacramentally, that is, in an unbloody manner, under the symbolic signs of bread and wine, but really. At Eucharistic communion, we receive "the Lamb of God who takes away the sins of the world," as the priest proclaims. We therefore receive Christ who offers himself to the Father in a perfect act of adoration:

> *The twofold consecration, that of the bread becoming the Body of Jesus Crucified and that of the wine changed into his Blood, symbolizes and realizes for the Christian, in time, in the depths of his heart as a child of the Father and of his will transformed by Chris-*

---

[178] Benedict XVI, Apostolic Exhortation *Sacramentum Caritatis* 66.
[179] Marie-Dominique Philippe, "Le Mystère de l'adoration" 36.

*tian charity, the divine reality of the mystery of the Cross, the
beloved Son's loving act of adoration. . . .*

*He is the one given, handed over. His presence to the Father,
that presence which is fully given to us, is indeed that of the Cross,
in which all is burnt up in love, in obedience to the Father.*[180]

From that moment, Christ can introduce us into his
adoration of the Father and take us with him into the act
by which he gives his Father the homage of all creation.
We then understand why Benedict XVI, in the text quoted
above, says that "Eucharistic adoration is simply the natural consequence of the Eucharistic celebration, which is
itself the Church's supreme act of adoration."

There is therefore in the sacrament of the Eucharist a
particular grace to make us go ever deeper into adoration,
such that adoration may take hold of our whole life and not
just the moments of Eucharistic communion:

*May nothing disturb the silence of my heart's cell. May I live there
with my dear Jesus in continuing adoration, loving reparation,
and in unending thanksgiving.*[181]

*Every day my soul feels the most pressing need to pray, to unite
myself with God, Father, that now I'm praying constantly. I adore
my Jesus there in the depths of my soul, and everything I do, I do
with Him and out of love for Him.*[182]

---

[180] Ibid., 43. See also what Benedict XVI says: "Jesus gave this act of obla-
tion an enduring presence through his institution of the Eucharist at the Last
Supper." "The Eucharist draws us into Jesus' act of self-oblation." (Encyclical
Deus Caritas Est 13.)

[181] St. Teresa de los Andes, Letter 44 of 22 November 1918 to Mother
Angelica Teresa, *Letters* 84.

[182] Letter 56 to Fr. Artemio Colom, S.J., of 29 January 1919, *Letters* 112.

Chapter 6: Practical Instructions on Adoration

The preceding chapters have essentially been a reflection on the philosophical, biblical and theological foundations of adoration. Their primary intention was to highlight the importance of adoration in the Christian life. However, learning that adoration is important is one thing, and beginning to live it is another. Experience shows that many people, even in the Catholic Church, are practically ignorant of everything pertaining to adoration. For this reason, I would like to end this book with a few practical instructions on how to live adoration. These instructions are meant in the first place for those who still have little or no experience of adoration.[183]

It is important to specify at the start that, strictly speaking, there is no method to adoration, in the same way that there is no method to prayer, because, more generally, there is no method to love. I shall simply give a few little practical means that might help one get into adoration.

ADOPTING AN ATTITUDE OF ADORATION

We have seen that the Greek word for adoration (*proskynēsis*) means "prostration." There is no doubt that performing this outward gesture encourages adoration. However, in practice it is not always possible to do this. It can

---

[183] Other instructions concerning adoration may be found in *Entrer dans l'adoration* by Caroline Schaefer.

then be replaced by kneeling.[184] Still, we should not abandon adoration in the places it is impossible either to prostrate ourselves or to kneel. Since adoration is first a spiritual act, obviously nothing prevents it being practiced in
planes, on buses, in trains, or in the office. But when we
find ourselves in a church or in our room, it is preferable
for inner adoration to be accompanied by an outward attitude that favors it.

As much as possible, retiring to some quiet (or at least
quieter) place will help us recollect ourselves. If we have
the opportunity to pass by a church, it will be good to go in
for a moment before the Blessed Sacrament, for this will
make it easier to adore. The sight of the tabernacle helps
remind us of God's presence drawing us to himself. It also
reminds us of the Lord's unparalleled love for us.

As adoration in spirit and truth is lived under the action
of the Holy Spirit, it is good to invoke him often and ask
him to *teach* us adoration,

HOW DOES ONE ADORE?

Here we recall the four aspects of adoration that we distin-
guished in the first chapter, but now to suggest a way to
live adoration. I will illustrate each of these aspects with a
few quotations from the Bible, the liturgy and the writings
of the saints that might help the believer adore, but all
people are free to express their adoration of God in a personal way.

The first aspect of adoration is the ACKNOWLEDGEMENT
OF THE CREATOR AS SUCH, and therefore also of our dependence on him here and now. For the Christian, this
acknowledgement can be done immediately by the act of

---

[184] In this regard, it is regrettable that some churches have pews that make it
difficult for the faithful to kneel.

faith, which puts him in the presence of God. We know that God is creating us at this moment and looks on us with love:

> *O Lord, you have searched me and known me! You know when I sit down and when I rise up; you discern my thoughts from afar. You search out my path and my lying down, and are acquainted with all my ways. . . .*
> *You beset me behind and before, and lay your hand upon me. Such knowledge is too wonderful for me; it is high, I cannot attain it.*[185]

This acknowledgement is accompanied by the homage due to God for what he is in himself and what he is for us:

> *For the Lord is a great God, and a great King above all gods. In his hand are the depths of the earth; the heights of the mountains are his also. The sea is his, for he made it; for his hands formed the dry land. O come, let us worship and bow down, let us kneel before the Lord, our Maker! For he is our God, and we are the people of his pasture, and the sheep of his hand.*[186]

> *Extol the Lord our God; worship at his holy footstool! Holy is he!*[187]

> *Bless the Lord, O my soul! O Lord my God, you are very great! You are clothed with honor and majesty, who cover yourself with light as with a garment.*[188]

The second aspect is the ACT OF LOVE FOR THE CREATOR. It is more difficult to suggest vocal prayers at this point, since love is such a personal matter. There are no two people who love the Lord in just the same way, and each love is unique in his eyes. Moreover, as for every interior

---

[185] Ps 139(138):1–3, 5–6.
[186] Ps 95(94):3–7.
[187] Ps 99(98):5.
[188] Ps 104(103):1–2. This whole psalm is praise to God the Creator.

prayer, adoration does not necessarily have to be expressed through vocal prayer; what is essential is the spiritual act of love for God.[189]

The third aspect is THANKSGIVING TO THE CREATOR for the gift of existence and for all our natural gifts, starting with our intellect and will (our spirit): "For you formed my inward parts, you knitted me together in my mother's womb. I praise you, for you are fearful and wonderful. Wonderful are your works!"[190] "Blessed be you, my God, for having created me!"[191]

The fourth aspect is the SPIRITUAL OFFERING TO THE CREATOR of all we have received from him: "Into your hands I commit my spirit";[192] "Take and receive, O Master whom I adore, all the treasures I have received from you."[193]

If we are before the Blessed Sacrament, we can take up one of the prayers of the Catholic tradition in honor of the Eucharist.

Adoro te devote, latens Deitas,
Quae sub his figuris vere latitas.
Tibi se cor meum totum subjicit,
Quia te contemplans totum deficit.

Godhead here in hiding, whom I do adore,
Masked by these bare shadows, shape and nothing more;
See, Lord, at thy service low lies here a heart
Lost, all lost in wonder at the God thou art.[194]

---

[189] One day, while St. Thérèse of the Child Jesus was gravely ill and in the monastery's infirmary, her sister Geneviève, who was watching over her, asked her how she prayed and what she said to Jesus in prayer. Thérèse answered, "I say nothing to him, I love Him!" (See St. Thérèse of the Child Jesus, *Her Last Conversations* 228.)

[190] Ps 139(138):13–14.

[191] Words of St. Clare on her deathbed.

[192] Ps 31(30):5.

[193] Elizabeth of the Trinity, Diary 153.

[194] Prayer of St. Thomas Aquinas for Corpus Christi: "S. Thomae Aquinatis Rhythmus ad SS. Sacramentum," trans. Gerard Manley Hopkins, in *The Poems*

Some Christians, having discovered the prayer "O My God, Trinity Whom I Adore" by St. Elizabeth of the Trinity (mentioned above), have learned it by heart, and recite it every day.

PUNCTUATING THE DAY WITH ADORATION

We have seen that the blessed and the angels in Heaven never cease adoring God "day and night" (Rev 4); they are eternally in an act of adoration toward God. For us on earth, it is not possible to be continually in the act of adoration, but we must tend toward this more and more by multiplying our acts of adoration throughout the day. In the story of Dom Belorgey, which we mentioned above, this Cistercian abbot suggested to each of his monks to punctuate each day with seven acts of adoration. This is a good suggestion. Do practicing Muslims not adore God five times a day, when they hear the voice of the muezzin? Why would Christians do any less? We could thus begin our day with an act of adoration when we wake up; by this act, we thank God for the gift of our existence, offering the day that is beginning to him and asking him to guide all our activities toward himself:

> *Lord, we praise you with our lips, and with our lives and hearts. Our very existence is a gift from you; to you we offer all that we have and are.*[195]

> *Almighty Father, you have brought us to the light of a new day: keep us safe the whole day through from every sinful inclination.*

---

of Gerard Manley Hopkins, ed. W. H. Gardner and N. H. MacKenzie, 4th ed., Oxford University Press, 1970, p. 211.

[195] *Liturgy of the Hours*, Morning Prayer, Saturday Week II of Ordinary Time,

[196] Ibid., Monday Week II of Ordinary Time.

May all our thoughts, words, and actions aim at doing what is pleasing in your sight.[196]

Likewise, we can end our day with one last act of adoration, offering to the Lord the day that has just drawn to a close:

Almighty God, we give you thanks for bringing us safely to this evening hour. May this lifting up of our hands in prayer be a sacrifice pleasing in your sight. Through our Lord Jesus Christ.[197]

The offering of ourselves in adoration enables us to enter fully into the "spiritual worship" of which St. Paul speaks in the Letter to the Romans:

I appeal to you therefore, brethren, by the mercies of God, to present your bodies as a living sacrifice, holy and acceptable to God, which is your spiritual worship.[198]

The other acts of adoration can be spread out over the course of the day.

ADORATION DURING MASS

When we participate in the Mass, the Church invites us to kneel, at least at the moment of the consecration,[199] to adore Christ really present in the Eucharist. There is no doubt that the moment following Eucharistic communion is a most special time to adore. We then adore Christ giving himself to us with such love, and we let ourselves be held by him and led more and more deeply into his adoration of the Father:

---

[197] Ibid., Tuesday Week I of Ordinary Time.
[198] Rom 12:1.
[199] In the United States, particular law states that the faithful are to kneel for the entire Eucharistic Prayer, if possible.

The divine Adorer is within us, so we have His prayer.[200]

If possible, it is good for us to prolong this time of thanksgiving after the end of Mass and let ourselves be penetrated by Christ and allow the Eucharist to bear more fruit in our lives.

We are to punctuate our days more and more with adoration and let it gradually become like the spiritual breathing of our souls:

> *I would like this to be the beginning*
> *of an endless act of adoration in my soul.*[201]

---

[200] Elizabeth of the Trinity, Letter 179 to Germaine de Gemeaux of 20 September 1903, *Letters* 128.

[201] Elizabeth of the Trinity, Letter 150 to Père Vallée of 31 December 1902, *Letters* 82.

Bibliography

Entries preceded by an asterisk are more technical and difficult in nature. The issues of the journal Aletheia may be ordered on the website www.aletheia.stjean.com.

"Adoration," *Encyclopédie Catholicisme*, vol. I, c. 157. Paris: Letouzey et Ané, 1948.

Ambrose of Milan (St.). *Expositionis in Evangelium secundum Lucam libri X.* In Migne, *Patrologia Latina*, 1603–1944.

Aristotle. *The Ethics of Aristotle: The Nicomachean Ethics*, trans. J. A. K. Thomson and Hugh Tredennick. Harmondsworth. Middlesex, England: Penguin Books, 1976.

* ———. "Metaphysics," in *The Basic Works of Aristotle*, ed. R. McKeon. New York: Random House, 1941, pp. 689–934.

Augustine (St.). *The Confessions*, Nicene and Post-Nicene Fathers, 1st series, vol. I. Hendrickson Publishers, 1994, pp. 45–207.

Bauckham, Richard. *The Theology of the Book of Revelation.* Cambridge University Press, 1993.

———. *Jesus and the Eyewitnesses: The Gospels as Eyewitness Testimonies.* Grand Rapids, Mich.: Eerdmans, 2006.

Beauvoir, Simone de. *Force of Circumstance*, vol. 1. New York: Harper and Row, 1977.

Benedict XVI (Pope). Homily for the closing Mass of the World Youth Days in Cologne, 21 August 2005.

————. Encyclical *Deus Caritas Est* ("God is Love"), 2005.

————. Post-Synodal Apostolic Exhortation *Sacramentum Caritatis* on the Eucharist, Source and Summit of the Life and Mission of the Church, 2007.

————. Encyclical *Spe Salvi* ("Saved in Hope"), 2007.

Cherif, Mamady Alkaly, "*Prière et adoration en Islam*," in *Aletheia* 12 (*L'Adoration*), déc. 1997, pp. 109–114.

Conde, Gloria. *Audrey: The True Story of a Child's Heroic Journey of Faith*. Circle Press, 2008.

Elizabeth of the Trinity. *I Have Found God: Complete Works*, Vol. I, trans. Aletheia Kane. Washington, D.C.: ICS Publications, 1984.

————. *I Have Found God: Complete Works*, Vol. II: Letters from Carmel, trans. Anne Englund Nash. Washington, D.C.: Institute of Carmelite Studies, 1995.

Goutierre, Marie-Dominique. "Adoration et contemplation philosophique," *Aletheia* 12 ("*L'adoration*," déc. 1997), pp. 47–60.

————. *L'Homme face à sa mort: L'Absurde ou le salut?* Paris: Parole et Silence, 2004.

* Greeven, Heinrich. "προσκυνέω (proskuneō)," in *Theological Dictionary of the New Testament*, vol. VI. Grand Rapids, Mich.: Eerdmans, 1995, pp. 758–766.

John Paul II (Pope). Apostolic Letter *Orientale Lumen* ("Light from the East"), 1995.

————. Encyclical *Ecclesia de Eucharistia* ("The Church Draws Her Life from the Eucharist"), 2003.

Jomier, Jacques. "L'Adoration dans le monde musulman" *Aletheia* 12 ("*L'Adoration*," déc. 1997), pp. 99–107.

La Potterie, Ignace de. "Jésus et les Samaritains (Jn 4, 5–42)," in *Assemblées du Seigneur* 16 (1971), pp. 34–49.

————. *La Vérité dans saint Jean*, 2 vols. *Analecta Biblica* 73–74. Rome: Pontifical Biblical Institute, 1977.

————. "'Nous adorons, nous, ce que nous connaissons,

car le salut vient des Juifs'. Histoire de l'exégèse et interprétation de Jn 4, 22," *Biblica* 64 (1983), pp. 74–115.

* Lassus, Alain-Marie de. *Chemins à travers l'Apocalypse. Études de théologie biblique sur l'Apocalypse de saint Jean.* Paris: Parole et Silence, 2012.

———. *Les Vertus théologales.* Paris: Parole et Silence, 2009.

Léon-Dufour, Xavier. *Lecture de l'évangile selon Jean*, vol. I. Paris: Seuil, 1988.

Origen. *Commentaire sur Saint Jean III*, Greek text, foreword, trans. and notes by Cécile Blanc. *Sources chrétiennes* 222. Paris: Cerf, 1975.

Paul VI (Pope). Encyclical *Mysterium Fidei* on the Holy Eucharist, 1965.

Philippe, Marie-Dominique. *De l'être à Dieu. De la philosophie première à la sagesse.* Paris: Téqui, 1977.

———. *I Thirst: Conferences on the Wisdom of the Cross.* Congregation of St. John, 1997.

———. "*Le Mystère de l'adoration,*" in *Aletheia* 12 (*L'Adoration*), pp. 34–35.

———. *Retracing Reality: A Philosophical Itinerary.* London: T&T Clark 1999.

———. *Retour à la source.* vol II. *De la science à la sagesse, itinéraire inachevé.* Paris: Fayard, 2009.

———. *Wherever He Goes: A Retreat on the Gospel of John.* Laredo, Tex.: Congregation of St. John, 2001.

———. *You Shall Worship One God: The Mystery of Loving Sacrifice in Salvation History.* Charlotte, N.C.: Saint Benedict Press, 2010.

Plotinus. *The Essential Plotinus: Representative Treatises from the Enneads*, ed. amd trans. Elmer O'Brien. Indianapolis, Ind.: Hackett Publishing Company, 1964.

Ratzinger, Joseph. *The Spirit of the Liturgy*, trans. John Saward. San Francisco: Ignatius Press, 2000.

Richard of Saint Victor. *In Apocalypsim Joannis*. In Migne, *Patrologia Latina* 196.

Rouvillois, Samuel. *Corps et sagesse. Philosophie de la liturgie*. Paris: Fayard, 1995.

Rupert of Deutz. *Commentaria in Apocalypsim*. In Migne, *Patrologia Latina* 169.

Sarah, Robert. *The Power of Silence: Against the Dictatorship of Noise*. San Francisco: Ignatius Press, 2017.

Sartre, Jean-Paul. *The Devil and the Good Lord*, trans. Kitty Black. In *The Devil & the Good Lord and Two Other Plays*. New York: Random House, 1960, pp. 1–149.

———. *The Flies*. In *No Exit and Three Other Plays*. New York: Random House, 1989, pp 47–124.

———. *The Words*, trans. Bernard Frechtman. New York: Random House, 1964.

Schaefer, Caroline. *Entrer dans l'adoration*. Nouan-le-Fuzelier: Editions des Béatitudes, 2006.

Scotus Erigena, John. *Commentaire sur l'évangile de Jean*, ed. and trans. E. Jauneau, ed. *Sources chrétiennes* 180. Paris: Cerf, 1972.

Teresa of the Andes (St.). "Diary," in *God the Joy of My Life: A Biography of Saint Teresa of Jesus of the Andes*. Hubertus, Wisc.: Teresian Charism Press, 1995, pp. 181–311.

Teresa of the Andes (St.). *Letters of Saint Teresa of the Andes*. Hubertus, Wisc.: Teresian Charism Press, 1994.

Ternynck, Marie-Jérôme. "L'Adoration dans la Bible," in *Aletheia* 12 (*L'Adoration*) déc. 1997, pp. 11–31.

Thérèse of the Child Jesus (St.). *Her Last Conversations*, trans. John Clarke. Washington, D.C.: Institute of Carmelite Studies, 1977.

———. *The Poetry of Saint Thérèse of Lisieux*, trans. Donald Kinney. Washington, D.C.: Institute of Carmelite Studies, 1996.

————. *The Prayers of Saint Thérèse of Lisieux*, trans. Aletheia Kane. Washington, D.C.: ICS Publications, 1997.

Victorinus of Pettau, *Commentary on the Apocalypse*, in *Ancient Christian Texts: Latin Commentaries on Revelation*, ed. and trans. William C. Weinrich. Downers Grove, Ill.: Intervarsity Press, 2011, pp. 1–20.

Voltaire. *Oeuvres complètes de Voltaire avec des notes et une notice sur la vie de Voltaire*, vol. II. Paris: Firmin Didot Frères, 1843 [old ed. accessible through Google Books].